MILK

John & Sally McKenna

In association with
the National Dairy Council

Food Photography: **Mike O'Toole**
Food Styling: **Anne Marie Tobin**

Landscape and Farm Photo Credits: page ends **Clare Keogh** • page 3 **Clare Keogh** • page 4 **Clare Keogh** • page 7 **Clare Keogh** • page 9 **VectorPocket Stock Illustration ID: 826168326** • page 11 **Clare Keogh** • page 12/13 **Clare Keogh** • page 15 **Dora Kazmierak** • page 19 **The Pimlico Project** • page 20 **Clare Keogh** • page 21 **Clare Keogh** • page 22 **Dora Kazmierak** (top) **The Pimlico Project** (bottom) • page 23 **Jack Kennedy** (top) **Clare Keogh** (bottom) • page 24 **Colm Mahady, Fennell Photography** (top) **Dylan Vaughan Photography** (middle) **Clare Keogh** (bottom) • page 25 **The Pimlico Project** • page 41 **Clare Keogh** • page 141 page **Dora Kazmierak** • 144 **Dora Kazmierak**

Published by Estragon Press
1st Edition September 2020

ISBN 978 1 906927 24 0

GEA

CONTENTS

THE STORY OF MILK 6
MILK AND HEALTH 8
BUTTER 10
GRASS FED COWS 14
IRISH CHEESE 16
LIVING & WORKING ON AN IRISH DAIRY FARM 18
THE NDC & KERRYGOLD QUALITY MILK AWARDS 20
THINGS YOU CAN DO WITH MILK 26
BREAKFAST & SNACKS 42
FISH & SEAFOOD 56
MAINS 70
VEGETABLES & PULSES 82
BREAD 96
SWEET THINGS 108
DRINKS 132
INDEX 139

THE STORY OF MILK

Milk is the currency of Ireland's food culture. Milk and dairy products connect everything in the world of food. Milk unites the farmer in the field with the cook in the kitchen. It unifies the cow in the pasture, and the family at their table. The food chain of dairy production links everyone involved at every stage of its natural life – the grazing cow; the butter churner; the cheesemaker; the barista; the chef.

In fact, milk and dairying are much more than the currency of Irish cookery: they are the pillars of how Irish people have thought, acted, and measured their lives.

'What I now say to students is that whilst the official government emblem is the harp, maybe we should consider another – a cow – to mark the cultural and economic contribution the cow has made to Ireland through time,' says food historian Regina Sexton.

Bothar, the Irish word for road, originally meant 'cow-path' and signified a track which was the width of two cows. The concept of wealth in ancient Ireland was intimately tied up with the value of cattle and, in particular, the value of milk-yielding cows. 'We've retained a very societal ownership of milk,' says Professor Alan Kelly, of UCC.

An outsider to the society was described as 'ambuae', which simply meant the person was 'worth no cows'.

The authors of *A History of Ireland in 100 Words* put it quite simply: 'Milk has been central to the Irish diet and economy since the Iron Age.'

Professor Patrick Wall of UCD points out that 'In the Devenish research farm in Dowth they have uncovered a megalithic tomb and in it found some ancient and porous pottery which contained dairy lipid residues.' This discovery, says Dr Wall, 'demonstrates that the residents of the Boyne Valley were drinking milk 4,000 years ago.'

Milk was also central to Irish folklore: when a beneficent ruler ascended to power, it was believed that not only would the weather improve and the crops prosper, but the milk of every cow would also increase.

And whilst we like to joke today that the Irish have a descriptive name for every variety of rain that falls on the pastures, in past times there were multiple names for the different types of milk.
There was very thick milk, and milk that was not so thick. Milk might be thick, but flowing. Milk could be of medium thickness, and it could be yellow and bubbling, in which case it needed to be chewed.

The Irish obsession with milk proves a simple truth: milk is a magic liquid. 'The Irish are the greatest lovers of milk I ever met', wrote the traveller and writer John Stevens at the end of the 17th century. 'Ireland has an extensive history and folklore tradition in seeking to create meaning and understanding of milk's magical properties,' says Regina Sexton.

Milk is a culinary shapeshifter like no other, able to transform into multiple guises, to change density, to disassemble and then reassemble, to become sour, and yet be especially delectable when made sweet.

'What I love about the stories of milk's cultural significance is the fact that it was an art, long before it was a science, and it would appear to magically transform,' says Professor Kelly.

Milk is a magic liquid, and deserves to be rewarded with a lexicon that rewards its superb quality. Like fine wine, Irish milk is distinctive, complex, revitalising, renewing. Irish milk has a 'unique fingerprint' says Alan Kelly. The secret to producing milk of the highest quality is 'to preserve our family farm model', says Patrick Wall. Irish milk and dairy products offer us a sensual experience, however we choose to use them. Thanks to the loving and tender curiosity of Irish farmers, we can enjoy dairy products that are uncommonly fine. Irish milk is Grand Cru Milk, a noble drink, and it is the currency of Irish culture.

'It might be an idea to make Bealtaine/May Day a day to celebrate not just the energy of workers but also the ingrained, deep-felt and long-lived importance of cattle, milk and dairy products to Ireland and Irish communities,' says Regina Sexton.

Mayday, then, should really be Milkday.

Milk and Health

Dr Marianne Walsh (RNutr) & Caroline Gunn (RNutr)

Drinking milk, and creating dairy products from that milk, has sustained populations across the globe for many years.

Milk is a Neolithic food – it is estimated that milk drinking began around 7,500 years ago in central Europe and scientists have suggested that it was a survival advantage to be able to continue digesting milk for its rich nutrient content. This is referred to as 'natural selection', which resulted in a change in human gene expression that enabled dairy farming populations and their descendants, to continue producing the enzyme to digest milk beyond weaning.

Plain, fresh milk is a natural dairy product, composed of a single natural ingredient – milk. Although milk is pasteurised for food safety purposes, no colours, preservatives, sweeteners or other ingredients are added. As well as being an affordable, widely accessible and versatile drink, milk is naturally one of the most nutrient dense foods available and is an important component of a balanced diet and an active lifestyle.

Cow's milk that is commonly consumed in Ireland is generally composed of 87% water combined with macronutrients (protein, carbohydrate and fat) and a wide range of vitamins and minerals.

Milk is naturally rich in protein, generally containing 7g in a typical 200ml serving. The protein in milk is considered a 'complete' protein as it contains all of the essential amino acids. The protein breakdown of milk is approximately 20% whey and 80% casein. Protein has many important roles in the body, contributing to the maintenance of normal bones and growth of muscle.

Milk's carbohydrate source is in the form of the naturally occurring sugar, lactose (approximately 4.8g per 100ml). Generally, sugar is not added to milk unless specified in the ingredients list – for example in flavoured milks. Nutritionally, lactose is not classified in the same category as 'free' or 'added' sugars and therefore, sugar-reduction recommendations do not apply to the lactose in milk.

Milk is comprised of over 400 different fatty acids, giving milk its distinctive texture and flavour. The fat content of milk varies from 0.5% in skimmed milk to approximately 3.5% in whole milk. Apart from the difference in fat and therefore energy content, they are all natural sources of a wide range of essential vitamins and minerals.

It is well-known that milk is a bioavailable source of calcium, which is a key nutrient for the normal growth, development and maintenance of our bones. In fact, 99% of the body's calcium is found in our bones and teeth. But there's more to milk than calcium – with a daily glass providing us with 8 essential nutrients, each contributing to the normal functioning of many processes in our bodies.

The nutrients in milk contribute to the normal functioning of many processes in our bodies:

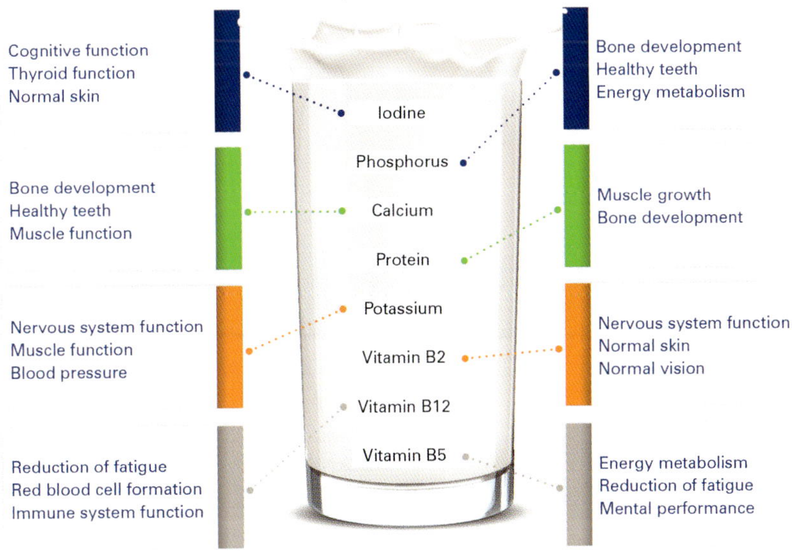

Source: EU Register of Nutrition and Health Claims made on foods

Dairy products, such as yogurt and cheese, are made from milk and, therefore, contain many of the same essential nutrients. For example, three servings from the 'milk, yogurt and cheese' food group provides 100% of the recommended daily intake of vitamin B12 and iodine.

Due to its unique composition, there also exists an emerging concept of the dairy 'matrix' which looks at how the various nutrients and components present in dairy products work together in synergy. This research explores how the health effects of these nutrients, when consumed in dairy products, may be more effective than the individual nutrients working in isolation.

Due to the grass-based production system, Irish dairy farms have some of the lowest levels of greenhouse gas emissions in the EU, with approximately 99% of the water used supplied naturally by rainfall. In addition, grassland soils have the ability to soak up carbon from the atmosphere and can therefore help to partly offset some of the carbon emissions.

Irish milk and milk products are considered nutritious, versatile and affordable foods and are well placed to play a role in meeting the global need for sustainable food production. This is why dairy continues to be included in dietary guidelines for sustainable diets.

Butter

Only in Ireland would you find a museum dedicated to butter.

It's in Cork city, on O'Connell Square in the Shandon part of town, an area that dominated Cork's butter trade in the late 19th century, when the Cork Butter Exchange was the world's biggest.

Butter was of such vital importance to the economy that Butter Roads were fashioned to speed the shipping of casks of butter to the city – the first Butter Road, built from 1747 onwards, ran between Castleisland in County Kerry and Cork city, shortening the journey from 102 miles to 66 miles, meaning a farmer could make the round trip with his horse and cart in just two or three days.

The museum celebrates an enduring companionship, both romantic and economic, between the Irish people, and their beloved golden dairy treasure.

'We've known how to transform milk into butter for thousands of years,' says Professor Alan Kelly of UCC. 'That it's so deeply ingrained in our DNA, going back that far, is remarkable.'

Butter was of such importance to the Irish that they surrounded it with superstitions: a milk churn had to be made from two different types of wood, and to counteract the evil eye of a witch who might have overlooked the cow and, thereby, stolen the butter, a twig of the rowan tree – the fairy tree – was attached to the churn dash.

A bachelor who came a-courtin' to the house should never lift the butter off the churn, lest it render the would-be suitor impotent. To deter the people of the Underworld, who feared salt and iron, the people of County Mayo would place a red-hot iron under the churn. Butter had to be protected, by whatever means. It was the mainstay of the Irish diet.

Historians have surmised that the Irish were making butter in the Neolithic Period, around 4,000BC, and in the Brehon Laws, butter was acceptable as payment for taxes and fines. To preserve butter for lean times, the Irish used the cool, antiseptic method of placing the butter in a bog, after salting and flavouring it with garlic, then wrapping it in sycamore leaves, before burying it in the bog.

A discovery of bog butter in Cullard, in County Roscommon, dated back to the sixth century and the Irish were preserving butter in bogs as late as the eighteenth century. The custom offered a 'high taste for Lent' as one traveller described the bog butter.

The modern Irish butter industry fashions butter from cows who graze on fresh pastures, which gives the butter a brimful of healthy fatty acids, along with a brace of Conjugated Linoleic Acids – known as CLAs – which help us to keep our weight down, and fight off cancer.

And those pastures gift to the butter a soupçon of beta-carotene, which gives Irish butter that warm, lovely, golden hue.

Despite its natural, health-giving qualities, for much of the twentieth century butter was forced to wage a war to defend its reputation. Proponents of a low-fat diet demonised butter, and their message persisted for decades despite the

fact that, as food and nutrition journalist Nina Teicholz points out in her groundbreaking book *The Big Fat Surprise*, the bias against saturated fats in food 'has never been based in solid science. A bias against these foods developed early on and became entrenched, but the evidence mustered in its support never amounted to a convincing case and has since crumbled away.'

Butter made a comeback worthy of a movie star, with *Time* magazine declaring 'Eat Butter' and the so-called science which had demonised it for decades was shown to be nonsense.

The latest research, published in *The Journal of Dairy Science*, concludes simply that 'dairy produce from pasture-fed animals is superior.'

GAA

Grass Fed Cows = Grand Cru Milk

When a research team led by Teagasc and UCC, working with the APC Microbiome Institute in Cork, published a two-part paper in *The Journal of Dairy Science*, in 2016, their conclusions were extraordinary.

The researchers' work revealed 'the scientific evidence to show the benefits of milk and butter from pasture-fed cattle in terms of superior nutritional properties, appearance, flavour and colour'.

Grass-fed dairy, it seemed, had not only won the Oscar for best film: it also hauled in best actor, best script and best design.

The research spanned a period of eight months of 'the real-time comparison of three distinct feeding systems widely practised throughout the world,' wrote lead author Tom O'Callaghan. Of the 54 cows examined, the cows on pasture produced milk 'with increased concentrations of fat and protein' and the milk had better nutritional status, and twice as many CLAs (Conjugated Linoleic Acids), which have been shown to be of major importance for our health.

When the researchers looked at the characteristics and sensory properties of the butter made from the milk of the cows who were on pasture, the grass fed cows again won the Oscars. The butters were nutritionally superior, had more CLAs, had a better texture, and sensory analysis 'revealed significantly higher scores for grass-derived butter in several attributes including "liking" of appearance, flavour and colour,' wrote Mr O'Callaghan.

Mr O'Callaghan added that 'pasture-derived butter is also nutritionally superior for heart health.'

The research confirms the assertion of Professor Alan Kelly of UCC that Irish milk has 'a unique fingerprint, because of the grass. The by-products of a grass-based system are the best bet for giving Ireland a unique terroir for milk.'

The scientists have discovered the workings of this unique terroir, but the poets have always known it. Back in 1977, in the introduction to her book of recipes, *The Ballymaloe Cookbook*, Myrtle Allen, the grand dame of Irish food, wrote the most celebrated aphorism about Irish food ever committed to paper:

'"The butter your sister is sending us is very good," I said to my neighbour one day. "Yes," he said, "that field always made good butter." '

Irish Cheese

Cheesemaking in Ireland is a craft powered by two sails.

The main sail is the large-scale production of cheese by co-operatives throughout the country.

The jib, then, is the cohort of artisan cheesemakers, working on their own farms, who are dotted throughout the entire country.

The history of Irish cheesemaking is an ancient story. The Irish word for cheese – cáis – is itself an ancient term, and throughout Irish history milk and milk products – referred to as bán bídh, or white-meats – were central to the traditional Irish diet. 'The close relationship between humans and cattle, sheep and goats, has long been known', write Kevin and Seamus Sheridan in their book *Counter Culture: The Sheridans Guide to Cheese*. New archaeological evidence suggests that 'cheese was at the heart of that relationship and central to what separated human farmers from other mammals.'

In addition to cow's milk, the Irish also milked deer, goats and sheep. From the milk they made a number of varieties of cheese, including tanach, a hard-pressed cheese made from skim-milk; and tath, a soft cheese made from heated sour-milk curds, which was likely similar to many modern Irish farmhouse cheeses.

There was also gruth, a curdy cheese made from buttermilk; mulchan, where buttermilk was beaten to form a soft cheese which was then set in a mould, and milseán, a sweet milk curd cheese eaten at the end of the harvest festival.

Cheese made its way into fable, and legend. The druid, Hui Lilaig, jealous of St Patrick's success as a missionary, aimed to kill Patrick by putting poison in a curd cheese. Patrick, wary of druids bearing gifts, blessed the cheese, which immediately turned into stones. Patrick, keen to drive home his advantage, then turned the stones back into curds, then once more back into stones, an astonishing dairy and geological transubstantiation.

Less fortunate was the great Queen Meabh, instigator of the great Cattle Raid of Cooley. Meabh, in her old age, was struck on the forehead by a piece of tannach – hard cheese – flung by her nephew, Furbaide, and perished from the blow.

And yet, despite this rich culinary tradition, the art of Irish farmhouse cheesemaking effectively disappeared, beginning in the 17th century. Political and domestic upheavals destroyed the economy, and embargoes were placed on the exportation of farm animals. Potatoes had become the staple of the diet, taking over the sustaining role of cheese.

On farms, milk was used to make butter, which was exported to earn much-needed income, and whilst some cheesemaking may have taken place in monasteries and nunneries, and in some of the houses of the wealthy, hand-made local cheeses vanished as a staple of the Irish diet.

The tradition disappeared, but it didn't die. In the 1970's, a small cohort of female cheesemakers emerged on the West Cork peninsulas, making cheeses from the milk of their own farms.

The first farmhouse cheeses created the signature style for the cheeses that followed: when your cheese expressed the singular place from which it originated, then you had made a successful cheese.

'Our formula is simple,' says Giana Ferguson, creator of Gubbeen Farmhouse Cheese, one of the first West Cork cheeses. 'The grass grows to feed the herd, their milk comes into the dairy, where we make cheese.'

It sounds simple, and it is, just as long as you have the skills and wisdom, and the determination, of a farmhouse cheesemaker. 'Making a living making something that matters' is how Veronica and Norman Steele, who created Milleens, the first farmhouse cheese, express the almost-vocational nature of cheesemaking. It may sound simple, but you need the soul of an artist to make a great cheese.

Today, you can travel to every part of Ireland and encounter an interesting, distinctive, local farmhouse cheese. The cheese revolution has been steady, democratic and passionate, and it has succeeded for a very simple reason: the people who make the cheeses do so on their own farms, so the cheese speaks of their land, their milk, their labour, their passion.

'It is mind-boggling to think that everything in a shop like ours comes from the same simple starting point: milk', say Ireland's leading cheese affineurs, Kevin and Seamus Sheridan.

'All cheese starts with the same magical white liquid produced by an animal... It is the ingenuity of the men and women who make the cheese that gives us the riot of choice. It's food with personality'. says Kevin Sheridan.

The cheesemakers have moved from being keen amateur experimenters to hard-working professionals whose labour of love produces some of the best known luxury food brands in Ireland.

In tandem, the success of the large-scale cheese production has grown apace, and you can fine superlative examples of Irish dairy cheddar-style cheeses in shops and supermarkets right across the globe.

Ireland's large-scale dairy industry is based on a number of seemingly irreconcilable elements, which ultimately work to its favour. Firstly, the suppliers are independent, small-scale family farms, from all over the country. 'Away from Ireland, people can't believe that Ireland has a successful dairy industry based on the idea of the small family farm model, and that we have managed to deploy a very high-tech, world-competing industry on the back of it,' says Alan Kelly.

Secondly, this high-tech, world-class industry is actually a seasonal industry. 'I don't produce milk 365 days a year, but I do farm 365 days a year,' says dairy farmer Vanessa Kiely O'Connor. 'The cows get at least an 8-week holiday from producing milk before they calve.'

Despite these seeming contradictions, Irish dairying has gone forth and conquered.

'Whilst most large companies in Ireland are science-based and international, dairy is really ours in the other direction,' says Alan Kelly. 'We're the ones who are owning the factories in England and across Europe and in the US, and that's still built on something that's a very old tradition.'

Living and Working on an Irish Dairy Farm

To live and work on a family dairy farm means living with - and working with - cows, and sometimes goats, and maybe a flock of sheep.

'I love cows,' says West Waterford farmer Tom Power. 'I enjoy working with them and getting to know their individual temperaments, and watching them grow and develop from calves to heifers to cows.'

This intimate life of dairying takes us back to the sagas of the past, such as the legend of St Ciarán of Clonmacnoise, who journeyed as a boy to study with St Finian, and who was accompanied on his journey by the prize cow of his family's herd, and the cow's calf.

At Clonmacnoise, Ciarán's cow produced so much milk as to be able to feed every pupil at the school.

As the cultural critic John Berger has written: 'The domestication of cattle did not begin as a simple prospect of milk... cattle had magical functions...'

Such as feeding everyone in the school with the plenitude of their milk.

In Ireland, cows observe us. John Berger also wrote that 'With their parallel lives, animals offer man a companionship which is different from any offered by human exchange.'

In many developed countries today, you can travel north to south, and east to west, and never see a grazing animal. That special companionship between man and animal simply doesn't exist.

'When I travel abroad people are baffled by the fact that the average herd size in Ireland is still about 100 cows, and most of them are family-run farms,' says Professor Alan Kelly of UCC. 'In its own way that's a remarkable cultural phenomenon.'

And so we are lucky in Ireland that we have preserved, through the aegis of the family farm, the fact that we can see the cows, and they can see us. This is important, because it is important that we care about animal happiness.

'I love them to bits from the moment they are born. They are my BFF,' says Vanessa Kiely O'Connor, who farms at Ballinadee, County Cork. 'Animal happiness is unmistakable... For any animal, happiness seems to consist in the opportunity to express its creaturely character...' writes Michael Pollan in his seminal book, *The Omnivore's Dilemma.*

And allowing an animal to express its creaturely character has practical results for our health. Cows are ruminants and need to graze. Allowing them to have space and grass and fresh water means that their milk is filled with healthy attributes that we humans need – conjugated linoleic acids; omega-3s; beta-carotene. 'I am proud to be an Irish dairy farmer... producing the best quality dairy products in the world,' says Tom Power.

THE NDC & KERRYGOLD QUALITY MILK AWARDS

Ireland's Quality Milk Awards (QMA's), supported by the National Dairy Council and Kerrygold, present a fascinating challenge for the judges who must decide each year who are the finalists and who – ultimately – is the winner of the prize which is popularly known as 'The Dairy Oscars'.

The criteria the judging panel employs is exhaustive. Milk quality is assessed for a full 12-month period, along with technical data. It's not enough for the farm simply to produce top-quality milk, as they are also judged on their environmental actions, and their dedication to animal welfare. Sustainability is vital, as these are family farms that must be passed on to the next generation in tip-top condition.

The judges must balance the need for an individual farmer to demonstrate innovation in the farm's dairying practices, whilst at the same time showing respect for the ageless Irish tradition of dairying on a family farm.

This is because there is a rather delightful paradox at the core of Ireland's dairying. This is the fact that this high-tech, world-leading industry is based on small-scale, intimate, family-owned farms.

The judges are looking, therefore, for the family farm that expresses the true culture of Irish dairying. Progressive, but always mindful of the family's history working the farm. Innovative, but within a culture that respects traditional methods of dairying. Globally successful, yet deeply-rooted in every field in every corner of the county and the country.

They want to find the farmers who believe in the magic of milk, yet who underpin their actions with the most up-to-date scientific discoveries. In a scientific age, the farmers are also aware that Ireland's dairy culture began in a pre-scientific age, when people began drinking milk 4,000 years ago.

The farmers need to know their cows, but they also need to know their fields and their grasses. And, if you can resolve all of these paradoxes, and produce a superlative quality milk, then you are exactly the sort of farmer who will be on the annual shortlist for the Quality Milk Awards.

From Farm to Plate – Quality Milk Award Winning Farmers

Patrick & Shauna Crotty

Patrick Crotty's 100 acres are way out west on the coast of Loop Head, the most westerly dairy farm in County Clare, with the beautiful, looming Loop Head lighthouse peering down on everything Patrick and his three generations of forebears have achieved.

Loop Head is more than slightly magical, the sort of unique region that attracts geologists from all over the world to study its rock formations, it's also a region that has its own hidden city – Cill Stuifín – which was submerged in an earthquake around the fifth century.

'Mother Nature dictates what we do,' says Patrick, so whilst the salty sea air gives his grass a tasty tang, too much wind and sea water will also singe the tips of the grass. 'You need to get the number of cows that is comfortable for your land.' To this end, Patrick keeps the number of cows relatively low – there are 70 cows in the Crotty family farm.

'Attention to detail' is Patrick's mantra – 'You keep an eye on everything you do with the herd' – and he praises the close-knit community and parish where he works, around Kilbaha. Tourism is vitally important to this part of the Wild Atlantic Way, so preserving the tapestry of the countryside is a key objective: 'You have to push the farm a certain amount, but you try and do it in an environmentally friendly way. Tourists come for the scenery, so you have to maintain the appearance of the place. You try to reduce your carbon footprint, and grow the best grass you can.' *Finalists 2017.*

Kieran & Ann Hearne

Kieran Hearne is typical of the modern, pioneering Irish dairy farmer, someone who can manage to improve milk supply whilst creating sustainable farming methods, innovating with new techniques, and also finding the time to be one of Ireland's top dairy breeders. Yet when his parents, both from farming backgrounds, first took over the farm at Ballinacurra, 'they had 53 acres of very neglected land in which ferns and scrub grew everywhere. There was only a dwelling house, and a small number of farm buildings, all in poor repair.' By the time Kieran came to take over the farm in 1993, after a year at Kildalton Agricultural College, the farm had grown to 72 acres, and all of Kieran's eight siblings had graduated from college.

Kieran's dynamism was there from the start: 'I was always passionate about farming,' he says, and his hard work has seen the herd grow from 27 cows and followers to a herd of 200. Kieran has a trinity of priorities for successful farming: 'The people. The animals. And the land.' His wife, Ann, and their four children all work together, carefully minding the animals because, Kieran says 'the animals are a fundamental'. He also minds the land and the environment: 'My job is to preserve the land, so we protect both the landscape and the environment continually.' *Winner 2019.*

Darran & Denise McKenna

'There's not two fields on a farm that are the same,' says Darran McKenna, whose farm at Derrygassan, County Monaghan, was the 2018 winner of the QMA Award.

Darran's secret is to know the fields as intimately as you might know the back of your own hand: 'What you do is you walk each field every five days, at a minimum once a week, and you enter it into your mobile phone so you know the paddocks that are growing a wee bit faster, those that are dry, or a bit damp, then you head to them when they hit the perfect cover.'

This ancient, field-specific specialisation means that Darran farms with a particular empathy for the health of his farm. 'I am always upgrading and planting new hedgerows and trees, even thinking of the bees as this year I sowed wild flower seeds as a trial and, if it works out, I will be doing more in the future. I'm setting up weed corners, sowing on the sides of laneways. You have to work with the land and the environment.' Darran has seen the results of his environmentally-focussed approach pay dividends, in particular when the water quality of the local lake was examined by the Blackwater catchment group: 'They couldn't get over the way in which the quality of life in the river bed had improved, and they were saying that this is proof of how modern farming works.' Creating a sympathetic environment in which to farm is personally important for Darran: 'You experience every season, unlike other people that don't realise a season has passed until they turn the page on a calendar - it's the circle of life!' *Winner 2018.*

Tom & Moya Power

Seven generations of the Power family have farmed their land in West Waterford, looking out from the Drumhills towards the majestic mountain ranges of the Comeraghs and the Knockmealdown Mountains. Today, Tom Power works alongside his father, Jim, who has walked the fields minding the herd since he was a boy of 14, more than 60 years in total. 'He has gone from milking a few cows, by hand, then worked through the introduction of rural electrification, into the modern era when we milk 290 cows.' Today, Tom stresses that farming requires an holistic approach, with animal welfare a priority, for farmers and consumers. Making sure the herd has the best grass to eat is pivotal: 'You're always trying to look for quality, so we're measuring grass every week. It's the same as checking your bank balance; we're just checking our grass balance, week by week. If I'm standing in a patch of grass and it's ideal for grazing, if you take a line from your heel up to your knee, it's a third of the way up from your heel. We're looking for leaf the whole time. And when we re-seed a paddock, we go for a mix of four or five grasses. It's all about the quality of what they're grazing.' Maintaining the health of the land, and protecting the aesthetic of the landscape, are also important considerations: 'We are working on a landscape that has taken generations to develop, so we want to do our part in maintaining it.' *Winner 2016.*

Vanessa Kiely O'Connor

'I wasn't from a farm,' says Vanessa Kiely O'Connor. 'When I took Ag. Science as a subject as a secondary school student, little did I know that I would end up loving farming so much that it was a career I became addicted to the more I learned!' Today, Vanessa grazes 65 cows on 58 acres of West Cork pasture near to Inishannon. As a female farmer, she says, 'I feel an extra bond, because cows are females. I feel I can empathise with them better.'

This empathy means that Vanessa is attuned to recognising what she calls 'behavioural stress' amongst her herd. Keeping the herd size small means 'all the cows know each other, and I have a bond with them, I'm part of their team and they know me. I love the old black and whites, I love their eye lashes, and they're so cute!'

Technology means that Vanessa can manage all aspects of the farming, allowing her husband, David, to work off-farm. 'It's all about the cow. Everything I'm doing is about her producing. It's about efficiency rather than expansion.'

'What we have in Ireland is an artisan product,' says Vanessa. 'Nobody can match us anywhere in the world because of our climate. I just love what I do.' Vanessa and her family 'walk every inch of the farm, appreciating not just the grass and the cows, but the life and nature that surrounds us. We even love the pesky rabbits who make Swiss cheese of our ditches and have eaten many of the trees we have planted. I feel every generation of caretakers of the land want to pass it on as good if not better to the next generation. That's what Irish family farms are all about. I'm sure it's in our DNA.' *Finalist 2011.*

John & Maria Walsh

All around the Walsh family farm, at Ballylooby in County Tipperary, the landscape is a pastoral idyll: winding, tree-lined roads, fields with gentle aspects, framed by friendly mountains, all picture-postcard-perfect. Seven generations of the Walsh family have maintained the farm, working together and bringing their collaborative skills to improving every aspect. John and Maria look after 130 cows, and 'I like to know my own stock,' says John. 'And if the children reared calves, they are always anxious to see how they get on as cows, and they might have a name on them, and that name will stick!' Looking after their patch of the Golden Vale means the Walsh family were 'planting trees and looking after hedges' before it became the established thing to do. For the family, any major event – the Millennium; a wedding anniversary – meant 'There was always an occasion where you would plant a tree,' says John, starting with the Eucharistic Congress in 1932. 'If you take down one, put back three or four trees,' says John. That's how you maintain an idyllic pastoral. *Winner 2017.*

Brochan and Joe Cocoman

'There is such a concept as happy cows, and I love happy cows! This is a true form of mindfulness and part of the excitement of farming,' says Brochan Cocoman, the inaugural winner of the QMA Award, in 2009. Brochan and his son, Joe, milk 120 pedigree Holstein cows at the family farm at Boherphilip, in County Kildare, and the farm was originally a stage coach stop on the Dublin-Cork road. Joe studied engineering in UCD, but realised that farming was in his DNA, and returned to become the third generation to look after their pedigree herd. In addition to winning numerous prizes at agricultural shows, Brochan and Joe are ever careful to 'have respect for the land, maintain hedges and cut at the correct time to protect habitats and nesting. This is the real essence of farming. At milk collection time when the quality and quantity of the milk meets your target, it justifies all the hard work,' says Brochan. *Winner 2009.*

Thomas Dwan

'They say I was nearly born in the parlour,' laughs Thomas Dwan, talking about his life-long relationship with the family farm at Bohernamona, near to Thurles in County Tipperary. Thomas was helping out in the yard after school, and even when he was studying at UL he was driving up and down to the farm to help out. 'It came as a surprise,' Thomas says of winning the QMA Award. 'All the other farmers were serious operators, so I couldn't believe it, it was a big shock.'

But it was the reward for some serious hard work on the farm, undertaken by Tom and his parents, as they grew the herd to today's 180 cows, improved the farm's milk quality, installed a herringbone milking unit, whilst also managing the total farm environment. 'The birds and the bees have a job to do, they play a part along the way, and you have to look at all the wildlife, so we try to work with it,' says Thomas. 'The land was there before us and will be there after us.' *Winner 2014.*

Kieran O'Sullivan

Kieran O'Sullivan milks 150 cows on 50 hectares close to Goleen, on the Mizen Peninsula in farthest West Cork. During Kieran's childhood, the family farm was a mixed farm – 'There were pigs and sheep and cattle, that was the way farms were back in the 1970s' – and over the last decade Kieran, his wife Catherine and son Cathal, have steered the farm towards dedicated milk production, in the process winning both regional awards and the QMA award for the

quality of their milk. 'The temperate climate of West Cork is favourable for growing good quality grass,' says Kieran, and the farm's proximity to the sea means there are rarely extremes of weather. 'To win the QMA award is the result of developing and improving the farm's systems year after year', Kieran says, and 'You must have a mindset to always do things to the best of your ability all the time, and you're always trying to produce the best quality milk.' *Winner 2015.*

Arthur, Ann & Conor O'Leary

'To us, dairy farming is much more than a business,' says Arthur O'Leary, who has been running the family farm at Leylands, County Limerick, for three decades. 'From bringing a newborn calf into the world, to seeing Irish dairy products in the supermarkets, our passion and grá for farming never ceases. We consider it a privilege to earn a living from something we really love doing.'

In addition to maintaining a pedigree herd of 108 British Friesian cows, Arthur and his son, Conor, have planted 16 acres of forestry, and created a 2-acre wildlife habitat. 'The pleasure of hearing the dawn chorus and observing various elements of nature on the farm every day never ceases to amaze us.' The farm also features an historic ring fort, which the O'Leary's have retained in its original form, tribute to their stewardship and determination to preserve and protect their land for the future. *Finalists 2016.*

Ian & David Lamberton

Ian and David Lamberton's farm at Castletown, Fahan, looks down on Lough Swilly, on the beautiful Fanad peninsula, in far north Donegal. It's an idyllic place in which to farm, and five generations of the family attest to the excellence of the land. The Lamberton farm has thrived because of the brothers' insistence that 'it's important to do the small things well: good hygiene, healthy cows and a good milking routine. These essential elements help create a great product.' With the next generation already involved in the farm, a family farming story that started back in the 1850's is set to endure and improve. *Finalists 2016.*

THINGS YOU CAN DO WITH MILK...

'Both physically and chemically, milk is a complex material,' writes Harold McGee, the esteemed scientist and food writer. Exactly. And it's because of this complexity that we are enabled to create so many different – and so many delicious – culinary creations, simply using milk as as our base.
Milk contains fat and proteins, it contains a wide range of salts, including calcium, sodium, potassium, magnesium and others. Milk contains all of the recognised vitamins, and it also contains lactose. Milk, in other words, contains multitudes, which is why it can shape-shift, thicken, curdle, change colour, become cheese, become yogurt, become a mother sauce, become labneh and paneer, become buttermilk and butter, kefir and brown butter. 'Milk is a highly complex and recalcitrant substance,' writes Pierre Broissard, and milk's mutations along the road from its natural state call for a poetic, sympathetic response from the cook.

BUTTER

If you over-whip cream in a mixer, what you get is simply butter, and buttermilk. For butter is simply whipped cream that collapses and separates into globules of butterfat, and the milk that separates from it.

Home-made Butter

Place 2 litres of room temperature double cream into the bowl of a stand mixer and beat – using the whisk attachment – at medium speed. The cream will be softly, then stiffly whipped, and then it will go a step further and separate into buttermilk and butter.

The next step is to remove as much of the buttermilk as possible, as leaving it in will sour your butter. Turn the mixture out into a large square of muslin resting in a sieve over a bowl, and press to remove the buttermilk into the bowl below.

Place the butter back into the mixer bowl, whisk again for a few seconds, to expel more buttermilk. Once again strain and squeeze.

Fill a bowl with very cold water and put in the butter. Using your hands, knead the butter once more, to remove more buttermilk. Replace the water and knead out more buttermilk. Eventually you will have a good butterfat mixture with no liquid. Salt the butter if you wish, adding three teaspoons to the mixture and rubbing in with your hands to distribute.

For spreadable butter, simply leave at room temperature for an hour.

Clarified Butter

Clarified butter, or ghee as it is known to cooks from India, is butter with the milk solids removed, giving it a higher smoke point for cooking. To clarify butter, melt butter in a small heavy saucepan and cook over a low heat until the froth rises to the surface. Simply skim off this froth and pour off the clear fat underneath, leaving any residue in the pan.

Brown Butter

Melt the butter over a low heat, watching carefully. It will foam up, and then the milk solids will begin to caramelise, which gives the butter its flavour. Watch carefully, as it goes from brown to burnt very quickly.

FLAVOURED BUTTERS

There are many, many benefits to making a flavoured, or compound butter, and perhaps the biggest benefit is the butter's ability to capture the energy of herbs when they are at their freshest, and at the height of their season.

A flavoured butter will last about a week or so in the fridge, and much longer in the freezer.

Having a flavoured butter to hand can lift many a workaday meal, help you to make a pasta sauce in seconds, or add a slick of magnificence to a steak, piece of fish, or roasted vegetables. Keep a box of different flavours in the freezer, and you can work your butter magic every which way throughout the year.

We are lucky in Ireland to have butter that is the envy of the world, and its golden hue and deep flavour is perfect for making these richly coloured and textured flavour bombs.

Compound butters are usually shaped into rolls, ready for slicing, and topping.

Compound Butter Master Technique

Take the butter out of the fridge to come to room temperature. If you have a dry flavouring, such as herbs and garlic, then you can mash the butter in a bowl, using a spatula. If you have liquid flavouring, such as lemon juice, Worcestershire sauce, Tabasco, then it's easier to use a food processor or, better still, a mini chopper. Either method, whip up all the ingredients together with the butter, so everything is combined.

The easiest way to roll it up is with some cling film, but if you'd prefer not to use plastic, then work with butter paper.

Mound the butter onto the clingfilm or paper, making sure to leave some clingfilm or paper free at the edges to assist with rolling. Begin to roll. Use a dough bowl scraper to push back any errant piece of butter, continue to roll it, while tidying up the edges. Then twist and spin the butter to make it tighter and tighter, compressing it until you have a neat cylinder. Place in the fridge or freezer to firm up again.

The butters will last a week or two in the fridge (if they contain garlic, the garlic gets stronger in flavour), or for months in the freezer.

Our recipes call for salted butter, but if you would like to take more control of the seasoning, then use unsalted butter.

Flavour Ideas For Salted Butter

Seaweed Butter
(great with just bread or crackers)
150g butter, 3 fronds of dillisk (the seaweed is best if put into a 170°C oven for 15 minutes to toast first), 1 tbsp chopped sea grass (ulva intestinalis), zest of 1 lemon

Pine Nut Spice Butter
(good with browned onions and chicken)
150g butter, 3 tbsp toasted pine nuts, 1 tsp cinnamon, a pinch of nutmeg, pinch of ground chilli and 2 tbsp finely chopped parsley

Mustard and Dill Butter
(good with any fish, or smoked fish)
100g butter, 1 tbsp Dijon mustard, 2 tbsp finely chopped fresh dill

Blue Cheese and Sage Butter
(good with steak)
100g butter, 50g blue cheese, 2 tbsp fresh sage

Ancho Chilli and Lime
(good with beans)
150g butter, zest of 2 limes, 1 tbsp lime juice, 2 tbsp Ancho chillies

Worcestershire Sauce and Chives
(good with grilled veg)
150g butter, 1 tbsp Worcestershire sauce, 1 clove garlic, 2 tbsp finely chopped chives

Gremolata Butter
(good with meaty stews)
150g butter, zest of 2 lemons, 2 cloves garlic, 2 tbsp finely chopped flat-leaf parsley

Tabasco Butter
(good on a burger)
150g butter, 1 tbsp Tabasco, zest of 1 orange and 1 lemon, 1 tbsp lemon juice, 1 tsp Dijon mustard

Tadka Butter
(used for flavouring lentil dhal)
100g butter, half an onion (chopped), 2cm fresh ginger (grated), 2 cloves garlic (minced), 1 tbsp chilli flakes, 1 tbsp cumin seeds, 1 tsp ground garam masala, 1 tbsp tomato purée

Irish Cacio e Pepe Butter
(good with new potatoes)
100g butter, 50g Corleggy cheese (grated),
50g Cais na Tire cheese (grated), 3 tbsp crushed black pepper

Garlic and Parsley Butter
(good for garlic bread)
100g butter, 4 cloves garlic, crushed, 3 tbsp finely chopped parsley

Herb Butter
(good with anything, depending on the herb)
150g butter, 3 tbsp finely chopped fresh herbs: parsley, thyme, dill, coriander, basil, rosemary, chives, tarragon, wasabi rocket, either individually or mixed. Sprinkle of coriander or fennel seeds, 1 clove garlic (crushed) 1 tsp crushed black pepper, sprinkle of chilli flakes (optional), and the zest of 1 lemon

Flower Butter

Another way to create a flavoured butter is to use it as a canvas for seasonal flowers: a flower butter. These butter creations can be spread out on a piece of pottery, some slate, or use a smooth sea pebble (which works especially well for a seaweed butter with wild sea flowers like the white flowers of scurvy grass, or the four-petal wild radish).

227g unsalted butter (at room temperature)

Choose any or all of the following:
handful of mixed fresh herb leaves
petals from edible flower (calendula, nasturtium, borage, violets, gorse, rosemary are all good)
coriander or fennel seeds
cracked black pepper
seaweed salad sprinkle
finely sliced spring onion
flaked sea salt (such as Achill Island salt)

Spread your platter or board with a thick covering of butter. A spatula is the best tool to do this. Scatter over the chosen ingredients artfully, and sprinkle flaked sea salt on top. Serve with good bread.

YOGURT

It is rewarding, and relatively simple, to make yogurt at home. Basically you need a spotlessly clean environment, a saucepan that is heavy enough not to burn the milk, and a place to keep it warm. Favourite spots include an Aga, a shelf over a radiator, a warming cupboard, a low oven, or a flask.

Ahmet Dede
Turkish Golden Yogurt

Ahmet Dede of Dede Restaurant in Baltimore, West Cork is a passionate advocate of local foods. To these he brings the technique of a Michelin-star chef. His food is also hugely influenced by the country of his birth, and there is a soulfulness to his cooking that complements West Cork ingredients.
To make his yogurt, Ahmet uses a local milk from Killowen Cottage – Holland's family farm, Enniskeane, West Cork – where Jeremy Holland is the farmer.

1 litre milk
50g yogurt culture or homemade yogurt

Bring the milk to the boil and immediately turn down the heat. Gently bubble the milk for 20 minutes, all the while stirring and mixing the milk with a ladle, time after time. By doing this you are steaming the milk and providing the conditions to expel the whey, and give your yogurt a thicker set.

After 20 minutes of gentle bubbling, turn off the heat and cool the milk down to 47°C. At this point, add your yogurt culture or yogurt to the milk and mix well. Put the lid on the pot and wrap the pot with kitchen cloths. Your aim is to keep the milk as close to 47°C temperature for the next 18 hours. If you have an oven with a bread proving setting, this is ideal. The next day open the lid and put the yogurt in the fridge. Let it settle there for at least 5 hours. After that you should have a nicely set, creamy, acidic silky yogurt.

Yogurt Made In A Flask

This yogurt needs no special equipment, just a large saucepan and a thermos flask. We learned the basics of making yogurt at Ballymaloe Cookery School. This recipe is adapted from one created by Eddie O'Neill, food specialist for the Dairy Research Station in County Cork.

1 litre fresh milk
15ml (1 tbsp) milk powder
15ml (1 tbsp) natural yogurt

Prepare a thermos flask, making sure it is spotlessly clean. We sterilise with a bit of Milton and then rinse copiously. You need to make sure there are no bacteria other than the yogurt culture, which would turn the milk. Add boiling water to the flask just before you add the yogurt, so you're adding the milk to an already warm environment.

Pour the milk into a heavy saucepan, and heat until almost boiling. Add the milk powder, stir well (adding milk powder enriches the yogurt). Turn off the heat and let the milk cool, until you can hold a soap-washed finger in it for 10 seconds without feeling uncomfortable. Keep stirring all the while. Finally beat in the yogurt.

Pour out the boiling water from the flask and pour in the milk. Seal and leave unopened overnight. The following morning you should have a nice set yogurt.

LABNEH

Labneh is a strained yogurt cheese that hails from the Levant region of Lebanon, Syria, Palestine, Jordan and Israel, and formed part of a mezze spread, eaten with a drizzle of olive oil and a sprinkling of za'atar spice mixture. As Jacinta Dalton's recipe shows below, it can also be preserved in oil.

Jacinta Dalton
Sheep Yogurt Labneh Pearls

Sheep milk has long had a sainted status for cheesemakers – in the 18th century Roquefort was regarded as the 'premier fromage de l'Europe'. Jacinta Dalton, Head of the Galway International Hotel School, shows us how to make a jewel of a dish with yogurt made with sheep milk. As the yogurt takes several hours to drain, this can be prepared the day before the labneh is needed.

800g Irish sheep milk natural yogurt
5ml (1 tsp) salt
250ml Irish rapeseed oil
sprinkle of za'atar or sumac, or wild garlic

Equipment needed:
Muslin cloth or clean non-lint tea towel
Piece of string
Sieve
Bowl
Kilner Jar

Add the salt to the yogurt and mix well. Place a sieve over a bowl. Dampen the muslin or tea towel and drape over the sieve. Pour the yogurt into the cloth-lined sieve. Gently squeeze the yogurt into a parcel, tie with string and place the sieve and bowl in the fridge for several hours. Whey from the yogurt will accumulate in the bowl, which can be used for fermentation, for drinking or as a cooking liquid.

When the labneh has formed, it should have a relatively thick consistency. The longer you leave it the more firm it will be.

At this point, the labneh can be shaped into little balls or 'pearls' and placed into a Kilner jar filled with rapeseed oil. Wild garlic can be added to the oil or fresh chilli.

It is important to fully submerge the 'pearls' and they will be preserved for up to 3 months in refrigeration. Please note: the oil will solidify, so take out of the fridge a few hours before you plan to serve.

Jess Murphy
Kai Labneh

Jess and David Murphy's Galway restaurant, Kai, is a west coast legend. Jess fuses Maori instincts with Irish ingredients, to dazzling effect.

500g organic natural yogurt
20g salt
2 lemons, zest and juice
3 cloves of garlic, crushed
extra virgin olive oil
olives
za'atar

In a large bowl place a large piece of damp cheesecloth. Make sure it's hanging over the sides so you can tie and hang your mix. In another bowl add the yogurt, salt, lemon zest and juice, and garlic, and give it a good stir. Pour into the middle of your cheesecloth, gather up all sides and tie in a gentle ball you can hang up.
Hang the cloth over a bowl to slowly drip overnight in a cool place or a refrigerator for 48 hours. Unwrap, transfer labneh to a bowl and serve with extra virgin olive oil, olives and a pinch of za'atar. It's fantastic with croutons or crackers.

Takashi Miyazaki

VINEGAR MILK
& COTTAGE CHEESE

Takashi Miyazaki, Cork's acclaimed Japanese kaiseki chef, recommends using milk in cooking for its 'kokumi' and 'umami', two naturally-occurring taste enhancers that magnify other flavours. Takashi also speaks of its health benefits, and the by-product of this recipe, milk vinegar, has 'great nutrition with calcium, magnesium and potassium - so good for recovery from fatigue and tiredness, constipation, high blood pressure, diabetes and dry skin. Also you can use milk vinegar for cooking – it has sweetness, saltiness, sourness, bitterness and umami.' Takashi adds 'You can use the remaining cottage cheese for salad, burgers, stewed dishes or miso soup!'

Cottage Cheese

1 litre milk
100ml rice vinegar

Heat milk in a saucepan. Take off from heat just before milk starts to boil. Pour rice vinegar into the milk slowly, and stir slowly. When the milk separates, then strain with a sieve and kitchen paper or thin cotton cloth.

You will get 800ml milk vinegar and 300g cottage cheese.

Cottage Cheesecake

2 eggs, separated
80g caster sugar
100g cottage cheese
100g natural yogurt
15g lemon juice
30g self-raising flour

Line the base and sides of a 15cm cake tin with baking paper.

Preheat the oven to 180°C.

Place egg yolks and 50g caster sugar into a bowl, whip with hand mixer until it turns white. Add the cottage cheese, yogurt and 5g of lemon juice and mix well with hand mixer.

Sift self-raising flour. Gently mix into the egg mixture with hand mixer.

In a separate bowl, place egg whites and remaining 10g lemon juice and whisk with hand mixer on medium until foamy. Gradually add the remaining 30g sugar and whisk on low until stiff peaks form.

Add one third of the meringue mix to the egg yolk mixture and fold in with the spatula.

Then add the remaining meringue and fold in gently.

Pour the batter into the cake tin and bake in the oven for 30 minutes.

PANEER

Indian Paneer cheese provides essential protein to those who adhere to a vegetarian diet. The cheese is first made into curds, called *chenna*, and then compressed and cut into cubes of *paneer*.

2 litres milk
60ml (4 tbsp) lemon juice

Bring the milk up to the boil in a heavy-bottomed saucepan, stirring often. Reduce the heat and add the lemon juice. Stir gently and slowly, and watch for lumps of curds to form. When this happens, turn off the heat and strain the milk through muslin. Hang up the muslin over a bowl for 2 hours to extract the whey, and then fold the muslin over the cheese to make a package. Place a weight on top and leave for a further hour to compress the cheese. Cut paneer into neat rectangles. It will keep for four days in the fridge.

HOLLANDAISE & BÉARNAISE

Both hollandaise and Béarnaise sauce use butter, emulsified with egg yolks, to make a luxurious sauce. Hollandaise is the simpler flavoured of the two, seasoned with lemon juice, whilst béarnaise uses shallots and herbs, and is acidulated with vinegar.

Brian McDermott
Béarnaise Sauce

30ml (2 tbsp) white wine vinegar
½ shallot, finely chopped
2 egg yolks
120g butter, melted
freshly ground black pepper
handful fresh tarragon
squeeze of fresh lemon juice

In a small saucepan, add the vinegar and chopped shallot, and place over a medium heat. Allow to simmer and reduce the liquid by half.

In a bowl over steaming water, place the egg yolks and whisk them. Then slowly add melted warm butter, whisking all the time, until you have a thick mayonnaise consistency, and all the butter is added.

Add the reduced vinegar and shallots. Season with loads of black pepper and freshly chopped tarragon. Add a squeeze of lemon juice. Set aside until you are ready to use.

Hollandaise Sauce

'It is probably the most famous of all sauces, and is often the most dreaded...'

So said Julia Child and her collaborators, Simone Beck and Louisette Bertholle, in their ground-breaking volumes, *Mastering the Art of French Cooking*.

Don't dread: hollandaise is straightforward, with one rule: only add more butter when the previous tablespoon has been absorbed. Slow, and gentle.

2 egg yolks
125g butter
5ml (1 tsp) lemon juice
5ml (1 tsp) white wine vinegar
5ml (1 tsp) mustard
salt

Place the egg yolks in a bowl. Melt the butter in a small pan. Put a small saucepan of water on the hob, and place the bowl with the egg yolks on top. Add the lemon juice, vinegar and mustard and whisk.

Add the melted butter in a very slow stream; if your little saucepan has a lip then use the saucepan, otherwise pour from a jug or add a tablespoon at a time. Continue to whisk between each addition of butter. When all the butter is added, you should have a smooth sauce. Season and serve.

WHEY

Milk gets rendered into 'curds and whey' after the milk has been curdled with acid or bacterial elements such as rennet, lemon juice, vinegar or yogurt culture.

Never throw your whey away! It has many, many uses – it's perfect as a marinade to tenderise meat. It's a source of lacto-fermentation needed as a starter culture to ferment vegetables, or to make sauerkraut.

There are cheeses that are specifically made from whey, such as ricotta or brunost, and it's used in lacto-fermented sodas and drinks such as Kvass.

You can use it to soak grains. Use in smoothies, or when making bread.

Whey lasts a good time in the fridge, but if you don't have any uses to hand, it also freezes well.

Aran McMahon

CAESAR DRESSING

Everything that Colleen and Aran McMahon cook in their Rua restaurants, in Castlebar, celebrates the rich artisan culture of County Mayo. Here is an ode to Mayo buttermilk.

50g Cais na Tire, Coolea or suitable hard cheese with nutty flavour, grated
3 anchovies
3 egg yolks
1 heaped dessertspoon Dijon mustard
5ml (1 tsp) Worcestershire sauce
2 cloves garlic
200ml sunflower oil
200ml buttermilk
lemon juice, salt and black pepper to taste

Combine all ingredients in a food processor except oil, milk and lemon juice.

Blend until smooth and, with the motor running, drizzle in the oil in a thin steady stream, taking care not to add it too quickly, otherwise it could split and curdle.

When the oil is incorporated, keep the motor running and add buttermilk, pouring steadily.

Transfer to a bowl and season and add some lemon juice to taste.

The dressing will keep, refrigerated, for up to 5 days.

Dress some baby gem or romaine salad leaves and top with some crispy bacon lardons, and shavings of a good County Mayo cheese.

RANCH DRESSING

'Enough! I grow weary of your sexually suggestive dancing. Bring me my Ranch dressing hose!' commands Homer in a famous dream sequence episode of *The Simpsons*. Ranch is the one true American dressing, the powerhouse of our Stateside cousins who use it with, well, everything: chicken wings; French fries; potato salad; pizza. Yes, pizza.

¼ small onion, very finely diced
¼ cup yogurt or soured cream
¼ cup mayonnaise
¼ cup buttermilk
30ml (2 tbsp) cider vinegar
1 clove garlic, crushed to a paste with a pinch of salt
fresh handful of parsley and dill
Irish sea salt and crushed black peppercorns
5ml (1 tsp) mustard

Put the very finely diced onion into a bowl of iced water for 10 minutes, then drain.

Mix all the ingredients together in a jar and combine through stirring and shaking.

Serve with iceberg lettuce salads, drizzle over anything grilled or barbecued, use in sandwiches, to dress bowls of chilli or as a condiment with burgers or chips, or use as a dip. Ranch dressing has many, many uses but, promise us: no pizza.

KEFIR

Kefir is a fermented drink, made from steeping milk with kefir grains, a gelatinous, cauliflower-shaped grain that is in fact a SCOBI – a symbiotic culture of bacteria and yeast.

approx 6 cauliflower-shaped grains of kefir
400ml milk

Place the grains and milk in a glass jar, and leave in the fridge for 24 hours. The milk will thicken and taste slightly tangy (not sour). Strain the milk to drink and reserve the grains to use again. They should begin to multiply. Do not rinse grains.

BREAD SAUCE

Bread sauce takes us right back, to the origin of food writing and the Latin recipe book attributed to Apicius. When Apicius fashioned a white sauce to be served with boiled foods, he added to his ingredients 'a few pieces of bread cut up to thicken'. Bread sauce has been on the menu ever since, and it is one of the greatest sauces of them all, and the one most beloved of children.

1 small onion, pierced with 4 cloves
bay leaves
6 whole black peppercorns
500ml full fat milk
100g fresh breadcrumbs
10ml (2 tsp) double cream
nutmeg
chopped parsley leaves
sea salt and pepper
knob of butter

Pierce the peeled onion with the four cloves and place in a saucepan with the bay leaves and peppercorns, and pour over the milk. Set on a low heat, and slowly bring the milk almost up to the boil, but don't boil it. Let it simmer for several minutes, then take off the heat and, if you have time, leave it to settle.
Strain the milk, pressing down on the aromatics to get the maximum flavour. Reheat the milk, scattering on the breadcrumbs and stirring them in until you have the consistency you like best, letting the breadcrumbs swell. Stir in the cream, grate the nutmeg and stir through, then stir in the chopped parsley. Season with sea salt and pepper, pour into your serving dish, and top with the butter.

CRÈME FRAÎCHE

3 parts fresh cream to 1 part buttermilk

Combine the cream and buttermilk and cover with cling film. Leave at room temperature for 12 hours. Refrigerate, where it will hold for about 6 days.

SOURED CREAM

450ml cream
2 tbsp buttermilk

Place half the cream in a jar with a sealed top. Add the buttermilk and shake well. Add the remaining cream, cover and keep at room temperature 24 hours. It will keep in the fridge for about a week.

BÉCHAMEL SAUCE

An easy ratio to remember when making béchamel is the 20:20:200 rule (gms:gms:ml), which can be increased or decreased according to recipe, ie 40:40:400 etc.

This is the ratio between butter and flour and milk. The process is always the same. Melt the butter then stir in the flour and stir until it makes a paste - also known as a roux. Slowly add the milk, beating all the while, and then cook, still stirring, for about 5 minutes to cook out the flour.

The sauce can then be seasoned and flavoured. Nutmeg is almost always used, along with salt and black or white pepper.

If using cheese, the rule is always to add the cheese at the very end of cooking. Too soon and it will split. Cheese béchamel is known as mornay sauce. Another well-known béchamel sauce is a simple parsley sauce. Make your béchamel as normal, and then add a good fistful of chopped fresh parsley. Other flavours for béchamel include saffron, horseradish or soubise (with grated, long-cooked onions).

OVERNIGHT OATS

This recipe for overnight oats is the tasty offspring of the original recipe for soaked rolled oats - Bircher muesli. These oats, soaked in apple juice, were first devised as an appetiser for patients of Swiss physician Maximilian Bircher-Benner. The original recipe was for oats, apples, cream and honey. Bircher Muesli has become a popular breakfast dish, and from this came Overnight Oats, a grab-and-go healthy breakfast option, where the 'cooking' happens in a jar overnight, as the oats are soaked in the liquid.

Our recipe takes the best of both worlds, the apples from Bircher, and the convenience of Overnight Oats.

Serves 4

100g rolled oats (not instant porridge oats)
185ml Irish apple juice
25g dried mixed berries
1 apple, grated on a box grater
150ml natural yogurt
seasonal berries or sliced stone fruit
honey

4 small jars, with lids

There are many ways of making this dish - you can soak the oats in milk, and add the apples later, or leave out the apples altogether, and use any fruit, including sliced nectarines, poached pears, banana or mango. We soak the apple and dried fruits overnight in the apple juice, so they don't colour, and layer the dairy element above, topping off with whatever fruit is in season, finishing with a drizzle of honey.

In a bowl, combine the oats, apple juice and dried berries. Grate in the apple (no need to peel), using the large holes in a box grater. Mix together well, and spoon into the jars. Cover each layer of oats with a thick layer of yogurt. Drop some berries or sliced stone fruit on top, and drizzle over a bit of honey. Place the lids on each jar and leave overnight in the fridge. You can eat one a day, as the mixture will keep for around four days in the fridge.

TURKISH EGGS

Some Turkish cooks like to add sage leaves to the brown butter, so if you have some to hand, then in they go. The dish appears complex, as there are three elements to the technique, but once you have it, then this addictive treat will be your brunch standby.

Serves 4

300g natural yogurt
1 clove garlic, crushed to a paste
Irish sea salt
small pinch of finely chopped fennel or dill fronds
60g butter
5ml (1 tsp) of Turkish Aleppo pepper, or chilli flakes, or 2.5ml (½ tsp) of sweet paprika
4 sage leaves
splash of white wine vinegar
4 or 8 eggs (depending if you would like 1 or 2 per person)
warm pitta bread or toast for serving

Stir the crushed garlic into the yogurt, season with the salt and the herbs, and set aside. In a pan, melt the butter and cook until it becomes light brown in colour (watch carefully so it doesn't burn). Remove from the heat and add the pepper and sage leaves. Leave in the warm pan.

To poach the eggs, bring water to a boil in a shallow pan, and add a splash of vinegar and a pinch of salt. Break each egg, one by one, into a half cup jug, or a glass, and pour the egg smoothly into the just bubbling water. Poach the eggs for 3-4 minutes.

Divide the yogurt between four bowls and, using a slotted spoon, place the eggs on top. Pour over the brown butter (now a lovely shade of red) and serve with pitta bread or, indeed, slices of hot toast.

NIAMH FOX – UPSIDE-DOWN PANCAKES

Serves 2

250g plain flour
50g rolled oats
10ml (2 tsp) baking powder
7.5ml (1½ tsp) baking soda
2.5ml (½ tsp) sea salt
50g soft brown sugar
550ml buttermilk
55g melted butter, plus extra for frying
zest of 1 orange
2.5ml (½ tsp) vanilla essence
½ stick of rhubarb, sliced very, very finely (very important as chunks won't cook on time).

Browned butter sauce:
100g salted butter
70g brown sugar or honey
50g water
the juice from the pre-zested orange

This is exactly the sort of dish that reveals chef Niamh Fox's punkish, idiosyncratic style of cooking.

Into a large mixing bowl, add flour, oats, baking powder, baking soda, salt, and sugar, and mix until thoroughly combined. Create a small well in the middle and add the buttermilk, melted butter, orange zest and vanilla essence. Whisk to form a lumpy batter.

For the sauce: Bring butter to a boil allowing it to melt and caramelize (it's important not to stir as you want the fat to rise and the milks to caramelise on the bottom). Once the mixture is light brown and smelling like caramel, turn down the heat and add in sugar, water and orange juice. Mix until melted and the butter takes on the consistency of syrup. Remove from heat and set aside.

Melt a small amount of butter in a frying pan over medium heat, and cook the finely sliced rhubarb for 1 minute. Remove rhubarb from pan, and keep warm.

To cook pancakes, add a little more butter to the pan, put a small spoon of cooked rhubarb in the middle, and pour about ¼ cup (30g) of the pancake batter over the top.

Cook until the edges start to set and the top begins to bubble, about 2 minutes, before carefully flipping the pancake – revealing the glorious rhubarb underneath. Cook for an additional 90 seconds to 2 minutes until the pancake is cooked through. Repeat with remaining rhubarb and batter. Store cooked pancakes in a 90°C oven until ready to serve.

Serve pancakes warm with browned butter caramel and some thick natural yogurt. The batter keeps well in the fridge for a few days if you don't get through it in one go. You can use any ripe fresh or tinned fruit to substitute the rhubarb if you can't get your hands on it.

BUTTERMILK FRENCH TOAST

Serves 2

3 eggs
120ml buttermilk
vanilla essence
cinnamon
8 slices good white bread
butter
icing sugar
bacon and maple syrup to serve (optional)

A new take on a classic child-pleaser, and a brunch staple.

Beat together the eggs and buttermilk and flavour with a few drops of vanilla essence and a pinch of cinnamon. Soak the slices of bread in the mixture for 10 minutes or so. Melt a large knob of butter in a frying pan, and fry the pieces until they are crisp and speckled with brown markings. Dust with icing sugar and serve with bacon and maple syrup.

RADISH TZATZIKI

250ml Irish natural yogurt
large bunch radishes
1 small red onion
1 clove garlic, crushed
15ml (1 tbsp) red wine vinegar, or a squeeze of lemon juice
5ml (1 tsp) sugar
Irish sea salt, fresh black pepper

This fiery riff on traditional tzatziki gives peppery heat and a hot snap of spice to the coolness of the yogurt. It's a sublime tension, perfect for grilled and slow-cooked meats.

Pour the yogurt into a bowl. Grate the washed radishes on the largest blades of a box grater. Grate the red onion on the same side. Combine grated radish and onion with the yogurt, crushed garlic, red wine vinegar or lemon juice, and sugar, then season with sea salt and freshly ground pepper. Place in the refrigerator, or set aside, covered, in a cool place to let the flavours get to know one another.

BRIAN McDERMOTT – PLOUGHMAN'S STEAK SANDWICH

Brian McDermott is one of the most highly regarded of modern Irish chefs, and all for a simple reason: Mr McDermott knows how to align tastes and textures to make food simply irresistible. Even before you get this elegant steak sandwich into your hungry hands, the scents and aromas will have driven you crazy with the hunger. And then: bliss.

Serves 2

oil for frying
2 x 120g sirloin or ribeye steaks
2 cloves garlic, sliced
fresh rosemary sprig
black pepper
40g herb butter (see page 29)
4 slices sourdough bread
80g pickle
2 slices cheddar cheese
Brian's béarnaise sauce (see page 37)
salad leaves

Heat a frying pan. Add a drizzle of oil and place the steaks in the pan. Do not agitate the steak, just leave it for 2 minutes, then turn it over. Now add the sliced garlic and rosemary sprig. Season with black pepper and add the butter, then cook for a further 3 minutes. Allow the steak to rest off the heat, then slice.

Toast the sourdough, spread with some pickle and layer with a slice of cheese and then some sliced steak, and a drizzle of béarnaise sauce. Top with a second slice of sourdough. Serve with salad leaves.

FETA DIP

200g Irish farmhouse feta cheese
½ cup natural yogurt
45ml (3 tbsp) olive oil
large handful of fresh mint, finely chopped
large handful of fresh dill, finely chopped
30ml (2 tbsp) nori flakes

Irish feta cheeses are vastly superior to the salty, rubbery imported brands sold in supermarkets, so search for these artisan cheeses to get the best result for this sublimely moreish party staple.

Place all the ingredients in a food processor and buzz until the mixture whips into a smooth purée. No need for salt. Serve with crackers and/or crudités.

QUICK ASIAN DIPPING SAUCE

1 packet of noodle flavouring elements
1 punnet soured cream
crisps or tortilla chips

This is a truly divine dipping sauce. It's inspired by a David Chang recipe from the first edition of the punky magazine, *Lucky Peach*. As Chang writes: 'You can thank me later.'

The recipe utilises the flavouring packet from instant ramen noodles or individual packets of noodle flavouring (you can buy these from an Asian store). These flavourings usually contain a mixture of seaweed, sesame seeds, and flavouring, such as wasabi or maybe bonito.

Open the flavourings and stir into the punnet of soured cream. Leave to settle for 20 minutes, and serve with crisps or tortilla chips. That's it.

CLODAGH McKENNA — CHICKEN LIVER PÂTÉ

Clodagh McKenna was a stalwart of the County Cork Farmers' Markets, selling her pâtés from a market stall, before she branched out to become a restaurateur, television personality and all-round leading light of Irish food. This pâté is wickedly rich, and wickedly good.

350g butter
500g organic chicken livers, cleaned
sea salt and freshly ground black pepper
30ml (2 tbsp) brandy
2 garlic cloves, crushed
1 dessertspoon finely chopped fresh thyme
30ml (2 tbsp) olive oil
200g wild mushrooms (such as chanterelles, morels or ceps)

Melt 50g of the butter in a frying pan and add the livers. Cook on a medium heat for about 15 minutes, stirring occasionally, and season with salt and pepper. When the chicken livers are cooked, there should be no trace of redness in the meat.

Transfer the cooked livers to a food processor. Add the brandy, garlic and thyme to the frying pan and deglaze all the juices from the livers (this is where the real flavour is!). Add the brandy mixture to the processor and blend with the livers. Leave to cool.

While the mixture is cooling, cook the mushrooms. Place a frying pan over a medium heat and add the olive oil. After 1 minute, stir in the mushrooms and season with salt and pepper. Cook the mushrooms for about 5 minutes, stirring to make sure they cook evenly. Remove from the pan and finely chop, then leave to cool.

When everything has cooled, slowly add the remaining butter to the food processor and mix until it has blended, then fold in the chopped mushrooms.

Transfer to a large terrine or 8 individual ramekins and leave to set in a fridge for about 3 hours. The pâté is delicious served with warm, crunchy, white bread or traditional Irish soda bread.

NIAMH FOX — IRELAND'S BELOVED JAMBON

Makes 12

2 sheets puff pastry

roasted red onion:

2 red onions, cut into quarters, then sliced
splash of extra virgin olive oil
salt and pepper
sprig of thyme, picked
small sprinkling of brown sugar

cheesy sauce:

25g butter
25g plain flour
250ml full fat milk
250g cheese, grated (Templegall, Gubbeen, Coolea, a good creamery Cheddar or bits and bobs from your fridge too.) Reserve a little to sprinkle.
pinch of nutmeg
pepper and sea salt to taste
200g of the best free-range ham you can get your hands on, cut into little cubes
1 egg, beaten with a splash of milk

Jambon is, of course, officially a 'thing' in Ireland, where we have taken these impish pastry parcels to our hearts. Niamh Fox takes the jambon into the culinary stratosphere using Irish farmhouse cheeses, smoked ham and caramelized red onion. Bring it on, says the nation. Veggies can leave out the ham, of course. For a party you could make these well in advance.

To make the caramelised onions: mix together the onions, oil, seasoning and sprinkle with sugar. Pop in an ovenproof casserole, set around 200°C for 30 minutes, then mix and cover and continue to cook for 15 minutes. Allow to cool.

To make the cheesy sauce: melt butter at low heat, stir in the flour and mix well until a dough starts to form. Gradually pour in the milk, mixing really well so that there are no lumps in the sauce. Once all the milk has been added, add the grated cheeses and a pinch of nutmeg, pepper and salt. Mix well until you get a thick cheese sauce. Add the finely cubed ham to the sauce, allow the mixture to cool.

To assemble the jambon: roll out the pastry, and cut each sheet into 6 squares.

Put a scoop of the cheese mixture in the centre of each square and a little of the caramelized onion, on top. Fold the corners to the centre and make sure they overlap (to avoid the ham and cheese from pouring out of the pastry). Pinch together the edges where needed. Brush the egg mix over the pastry and sprinkle the final bit of cheese on top, and repeat for the other squares.

Place on oven tray and bake at 200°C for 15-20 minutes or until golden-brown.

SEAFOOD CHOWDER

Chowder is enormously satisfying to eat, and almost as satisfying to cook. You need a mix of white fish, smoked fish, and shellfish, set against a tableau of slowly sweated vegetables, then plenty of milk and cream to supply that satisfying heft. If you have a gentle sea breeze available, so much the better.

Serves 4

25g butter
1 leek, finely chopped
2 stalks celery, finely chopped
1 carrot, finely chopped
2 large potatoes – about 450g – finely chopped
400ml milk
400ml stock
300g mixed fish and shellfish
150ml cream
chopped chives, parsley and dill
chive flowers to garnish (optional)

Melt the butter in a large pan, then add the finely chopped vegetables. Swoosh around in the butter, then place a large butter paper or circle of baking paper on top, turn the heat down, and gently sweat the vegetables until tender – this serves to magnify and sweeten their flavour.

Remove paper and add the milk and stock and bring just to the boil, then simmer until the potato can be easily squished against the side of the pot.

Add the seafood and shellfish mix, and the cream. Simmer until cooked, then stir in the chopped herbs.

Serve, garnished with the chive flowers, should you have some.

SMOKED TROUT PÂTÉ

150g hot smoked Irish trout
120g cream cheese, such as St Tola Divine
handful of chives, chopped
zest and juice of ½ lemon
15ml (1 tbsp) horseradish sauce
15ml (1 tbsp) natural yogurt
sprinkle sea salt

Smoked fish and Irish cream cheese, mixed together, are the epitome of culinary elegance and compatibility.

Flake the fish, then gently combine all the ingredients together. Easy.

FINNAN HADDIE

Serves 4

450g fillet of smoked haddock
500ml milk
pepper and salt
lemon juice
nutmeg
handful chopped parsley
knob butter
4 eggs

This recipe was given to us by Ken Buggy, one of the most idiosyncratic figures in Irish hospitality.

Preheat the oven to 220°C.
Place haddock in a small casserole. It should fit tightly. Barely cover with milk. Season with plenty of pepper, a sprinkle of sea salt and a dash of lemon juice. Add a pinch of nutmeg, some chopped parsley, and a big knob of butter. Cover the casserole, place in the oven and turn the heat down to 180ºC. Cook for 10 minutes. Remove from oven, and gently crack in 4 eggs. Return to the oven. Cook for 5-7 minutes and serve from the casserole.

MARY REDMOND — CRAB CAKES

These plosively moreish crab cakes, the signature dish of Mary and Cillian's much-missed Kilkee restaurant, Murphy Blacks, are also one of the culinary symbols of County Clare's Loop Head peninsula.

Makes 6

250g fresh crab meat
4 spring onions
½ red pepper
1 small red chilli
1 clove of garlic
handful of fresh coriander leaves
2 slices of bread made into fine breadcrumbs

white sauce:
20g butter
20g flour
100ml milk

15ml (1 tbsp) mayonnaise
juice of ½ lemon
salt and pepper to taste
plain flour
1 egg beaten with a little milk
breadcrumbs for coating

butter and oil for frying

Leave the crab meat to drain in a sieve for a short while to dispel any excess water.

Make the white sauce: melt the butter and stir in the flour, making sure there are no lumps. Slowly stir in the milk, little by little, and then simmer for approximately 5 minutes.

Finely chop the spring onions, red pepper, chilli, garlic and coriander in a food processor or mini blender, put in a bowl and then add the breadcrumbs, white sauce, mayonnaise and lemon juice, and then the crab meat, adding more breadcrumbs if the mix is too wet.

Shape into 6 golf ball-sized rounds and flatten slightly. Chill in the fridge to firm up.

Get a bowl each for the flour, the egg and the breadcrumbs. Dip the crab cakes into the flour, then the egg and finally the crumbs. Heat the butter and oil in a frying pan and, over medium heat, cook the crab cakes until brown on both sides and hot through.

Serve with chilli jam, mayonnaise and mixed salad.

HAKE AND PRAWNS IN SAFFRON BÉCHAMEL

This unorthodox béchamel, which features onions, saffron and lemon zest, is a terrific example of what happens when iconoclastic Catalan cooks – from the home of Miró and Dalí – get their hands on a traditional French béchamel.

Serves 4

750g white fish fillets, such as hake or cod
150g prawns and/or scallops
olive oil for frying the fish

100g butter
1 onion, finely sliced
75g flour
650ml milk
saffron threads, a pinch
grated zest of 1 lemon
Irish sea salt and freshly ground pepper
75g breadcrumbs

Turn your oven to 190°C.

In a large frying pan, melt 75g of butter and sauté the finely sliced onion until golden and translucent (about 4-5 minutes). Stir in the flour, then gradually add the milk and slowly bring to the boil, stirring the whole time, for about 5 minutes, until the sauce thickens.

When thick, and the flour is cooked, turn down the heat, add the saffron threads and lemon zest. Season with salt and freshly ground pepper.

Sauté the prawns or scallops in the oil, for one minute, then place in a casserole dish. Season the fillets of fish with salt and pepper and sauté in the same pan, adding a little more oil if needed. Turn the fish, and cook on the second side for a couple of minutes. Place in the casserole with the prawns or scallops.

In a different saucepan, melt the remaining butter, stir in the breadcrumbs and gently brown.

Pour the sauce in and around and over the fish and shellfish, and top with the breadcrumbs.

Bake in the oven for about 15 minutes.

BAKED PLAICE WITH CHERRY TOMATOES

Sweet fish, sweet and tart tomatoes, comforting rich cream, topped with a confetti of cheese that provides the bass line for the quartet. Sheer comfort on a plate.

Serves 4

4 plaice fillets
salt and pepper
25g butter
12 cherry tomatoes, kept whole
200ml crème fraîche
100g hard, grating cheese such as Cais na Tire or Parmesan, freshly grated

Preheat the oven to 200°C.

Butter a baking tray. Season the plaice with the salt and pepper and lay, skin side down, on the tray. (Use baking paper, if you wish.)

Dot with the tomatoes.

Drizzle over crème fraîche and sprinkle over the cheese.

Bake for approximately 12 minutes.

MUSSEL & POTATO SALAD

SERVES 4

ranch dressing:
¼ small onion, very finely diced
¼ cup yogurt or soured cream
¼ cup mayonnaise
¼ cup buttermilk
30ml (2 tbsp) cider vinegar
1 clove garlic, crushed to a paste with a pinch of salt
fresh handful of parsley and dill
Irish sea salt and crushed black peppercorns
5ml (1 tsp) mustard

salad:
500g new potatoes in their skins
100ml white wine, cider or kombucha
1kg mussels in shells
mixed washed salad leaves, herbs and edible flowers

Mussels and potatoes are heavenly bedfellows – just think of the glory that is the national dish of Belgium, moules et frites.

To make the dressing: put the very finely diced onion into a bowl of iced water for 10 minutes, then drain.

Mix all the ingredients together in a jar and combine through stirring and shaking.

Wash the potatoes, and steam until just soft.

In another large saucepan, heat the wine, cider or kombucha and tip in your mussels. When the mussels open, remove from the heat and strain, reserving the sauce.

Toss the cooked, still warm, potatoes in the mussel liquid and ranch dressing. Then, gently toss together the potatoes with mussels.

Serve on a platter of salad leaves and herbs, with extra dressing on the side.

SEAFOOD CRUMBLE

Serves 4

velouté sauce:
1 litre fish stock
225ml cream
30g softened butter
30g flour

seafood mixture:
900g fresh white fish and seafood that has been skinned, boned and cut into cubes
200g carrot, peeled and grated
150g leek, finely chopped

crumble topping:
100g butter
2 cloves garlic, minced
150g breadcrumbs
2 tablespoons chopped fresh parsley

We learned the recipe for Seafood Crumble from chef Martin Shanahan, of Kinsale's Fishy Fishy, first published in the little book of *Irish Seafood Cookery.* Martin's secret is to add the raw carrot and leek, which stay crisp and fresh in the recipe.

Preheat the oven to 180°C. Make a velouté sauce by bringing the stock and cream to the boil in a pan. Mix together the butter and the flour, and beat this roux, small piece by small piece, into the liquid. Stir until the sauce thickens.

Steam the fish until just cooked. Grate the carrot, and finely slice the leek.

For the crumble topping, melt the butter with the garlic for the crumble topping, then stir the breadcrumbs and the parsley into the garlic butter.

Assemble the dish in an ovenproof casserole: gently stir the fish and vegetables into the sauce and pour into the casserole. Top with the garlic breadcrumbs. Bake for 20 minutes until golden.

TONY DAVIDSON — CRISPY HADDOCK GOUJONS

Tony Davidson cooks seafood for the gods from his little galley of a kitchen at Fisk at Downings, in north Donegal. This is Tony's battered fish, and the secret is the buttermilk.

Serves 2 as a snack

250g haddock
235ml buttermilk

batter:
100g flour
100g cornflour
10g cayenne
10g smoked paprika

500ml oil for frying

garnish:
2 spring onions, thinly sliced
2 red chillies, thinly sliced
sea salt, black pepper

dip:
200g natural yogurt
juice 1 lemon

Cut the haddock into strips, roughly finger sized. Cover the haddock in buttermilk and leave for 20 minutes. Mix the flour, cornflour and spices together.

Heat oil to 190°C in a deep-fat fryer.

Drain the haddock and coat strips in the flour mix, about 4 strips at a time, and add them to the oil, cooking for around 4 minutes each until golden brown.

Once all the haddock strips have been cooked, transfer them to a serving bowl, and add thinly sliced spring onion and chillies. Season with a generous amount of sea salt and black pepper.

Mix the yogurt with lemon juice and season, then serve on the side as a dip.

TURKEY MEATBALLS

Serves 4

500g turkey, minced
½ cup milk
1 cup white breadcrumbs
1 onion, grated
1 stick celery, grated
1 egg, beaten
45ml (3 tbsp) ras el hanout spice mix
sea salt and black pepper

braising sauce:
1 onion, finely sliced
15ml (1 tbsp) olive oil
2 cloves garlic, crushed
pinch chilli flakes
350ml chicken stock
2 dried limes (optional)
200g frozen peas

yogurt sauce:
1 egg yolk
15ml (1 tbsp) cornflour
150g natural yogurt
coriander leaves, chopped

Here turkey is fashioned into meatballs, with a rich Middle Eastern yogurt sauce. The option of dried limes, a staple of Iranian cooking (available from Asian shops) brings a touch of perfumed genius to the sauce.

Preheat oven to 190°C.

Put the turkey mince into a bowl. In a separate bowl, pour milk over breadcrumbs to soften. Add breadcrumbs to turkey mince, together with onion, celery, egg and ras el hanout spices, and season with salt and pepper. With wet hands, form mixture into golf ball-sized meatballs, and place on an oiled baking tray. Bake in the oven for 10 minutes while you make the braising sauce.

Sauté the onion in oil until translucent, then add the crushed garlic and cook for a few more minutes, adding the pinch of chilli flakes. Pour in the stock, pierce the dried limes with a sharp knife and add to the stock. Simmer for 5 minutes, then add the meatballs. Simmer for 20 minutes, then add the frozen peas.

Stir the egg yolk and cornflour into the yogurt. Slowly add the yogurt mixture to the meatballs, stirring all the while. Simmer for a couple of minutes, scatter over the chopped coriander leaves, then plate up.

RICOTTA-STUFFED SPATCHCOCKED ROAST CHICKEN

Placing the stuffing under the skin makes for wonderfully moist chicken flesh. The spatchcocking technique is simple: you only need a good kitchen knife.

Serves 4

1 large free-range chicken
Irish sea salt and pepper
100g ricotta
50g pesto
butter

Preheat the oven to 220°C.

Prepare the chicken by cutting on either side of the backbone with a very sharp knife, or poultry scissors. Save the backbone for stock. Using the flat of your hand, press down on the chicken until it flattens out, then scatter seasoning on the underside. Starting at the opposite end from the wishbone, slide your fingers under the chicken skin and gently prise it up to offer two deep pockets atop the breasts. Drain the ricotta for several minutes in a sieve, then season with salt and pepper and mix with the pesto. Using your fingers, carefully pack the stuffing mixture under the skin on either side of the breast bone, extending down over the thighs and drumsticks.

Rub butter over the chicken skin, place in the preheated oven and, after 20 minutes, reduce the heat to 180°C, and roast for a further 30 minutes, at which point it is time to check the temperature of the bird. A good-quality chicken will be completely cooked when the temperature on your meat probe reads 70°C, and as you let the chicken rest the temperature will continue to rise by 2-3 degrees. If you don't have a meat thermometer, then stick a knife into one of the chicken legs, and look for the juices to run clear.

Allow the chicken to rest for at least 10 minutes before carving.

CAITLIN RUTH – CHICKEN EMPANADAS

Empanadas are the famous hand-held pastry pies of Latin America, found in multiple styles all the way from Los Angeles through Mexico, Brazil and into the Latin Caribbean. Whilst the celebrated chef Caitlin Ruth hails from a little north of that region – Ms Ruth is from Dublin, New Hampshire – she has an innate affinity with these sublime pies.

pastry:

2 cups strong white flour
5 ml (1 tsp) sea salt
5ml (1 tsp) white sugar
70g cold butter, cubed
1 egg
⅓ cup cold milk

filling:

2 onions, finely chopped and sautéed until soft
250g cooked chicken, finely chopped
a handful of capers
a handful of pitted green olives, chopped
a handful of raisins
pinch of oregano
squeeze of lemon
salt and chilli flakes

spicy milk mojo:

300ml whole milk
6 spring onions, chopped
4 garlic cloves, peeled
2.5ml (½ tsp) cumin seeds
2.5ml (½ tsp) sea salt
big handful of fresh coriander, stalks and all
2 big spicy green chilies
½ green pepper, chopped roughly

Pulse the flour, salt and sugar in a food processor, then pulse in the cubed butter. Finally pulse in the egg and cold milk until just combined.

Form the dough into a disc, wrap, and chill until needed.

Mix all the filling ingredients in a bowl, taste and season. This doesn't have to be very spicy, because the milk mojo will be.

Keep refrigerated while you roll out the pastry very thinly, then cut into 7.5cm rounds. The pastry should be very thin, so you can give each round a further little roll at this point. Put a little bit of water or egg wash around the outside perimeter of half the pastry round, then hold the round in your left hand. Put a hefty spoon of filling into the middle of the round, and with your right hand, pinch up the sides of the pastry round, until they meet, forming a half moon. Pinch the edges into a cute little design, which you'll surely master by the last one. Set aside on a floured tea towel. When you've made them all, you can either deep or shallow fry (preferred), or bake (egg wash them first) in a 180°C oven until golden brown. Serve with ramekins of Spicy Milk Mojo: place all the ingredients in a jug, and then blend with a hand blender until smooth and green. Serve in ramekins as a dip for the empanadas, or drizzle on anything! Also makes a lovely dressing for a spicy, chopped salad.

BOLOGNAISE SAUCE

'One of the most satisfying experiences accessible to the sense of taste' was how Marcella and Victor Hazan describe Ragu, the notoriously delicious sauce which the people of Bologna claim cannot be made correctly anywhere else. With due respect to that city's great culinary culture, they are dead wrong. The secret of a great ragu is slow, steady simmering, for hours on end, and the use of milk, so that you achieve, finally, that voluptuous slinkiness that begs to cling to a ribbon of pasta.

Serves 4

45ml (3 tbsp) olive oil
50g butter
1 onion, chopped
2 carrots, chopped
2 sticks celery, chopped
salt and pepper
grated nutmeg
500g minced beef
400g tin tomatoes
stock or water
150ml milk

In a heavy pot, heat the oil and butter and add the onion. Sauté until it changes colour, and then add the carrots and celery, season with salt, pepper and nutmeg, and sauté until they too begin to soften. Add the minced beef, and cook until it changes colour, stirring all the time. Stir in the tomatoes, then rinse out the tomato tin – half fill with water or stock – and add to the saucepan. Finally add the milk, stirring it into the sauce.

Leave the pot on a low heat, simmering, for 3 hours, leaving the pot uncovered for the first hour.

LAMBS' KIDNEYS WITH JUNIPER

This could be eaten for a very late breakfast, in the Edwardian style, or for dinner, in the modern age. Kidneys, and other offal delights, have fast fallen out of fashion, so let's eat up and make them hip and happening again.

Serves 4

8 lambs' kidneys
4 juniper berries
salt
freshly ground black pepper
25g butter
15ml (1 tbsp) wholegrain mustard
200ml cream
handful chopped parsley

Skin and halve the kidneys horizontally, and cut out the inner cores (you can ask your butcher to do this for you).

Pound the juniper berries with some salt and pepper in a mortar with pestle, and rub this mixture into the kidneys.

Melt the butter and sauté the kidneys for 4 minutes before adding the mustard and cream. Increase the heat and cook until the sauce thickens.

Sprinkle with parsley and serve.

DONAL SKEHAN — THREE CHEESE BAKED GNOCCHI

This seemingly simple dish shows the way in which Donal Skehan's flavour-filled cooking is built up of small steps which maximise flavour. Look at how Donal seasons the oil with the garlic, enriches the dish with cream, freshens it up with spinach, then mixes the trio of cheeses so the gnocchi has a rich overcoat in which to bathe. Simple, smart.

Serves 4

500g best quality store bought gnocchi
salt
45ml (3 tbsp) extra virgin olive oil
6 cloves garlic, finely sliced
5ml (1 teasp) chilli flakes
700g tomato passata
50ml cream
75g baby spinach
handful of basil leaves
75g blue cheese, crumbled
75g ricotta
50g Parmesan cheese, grated (or Cais na Tire)

Preheat the oven to 200°C. Cook the gnocchi in boiling salted water for 2-3 minutes before draining under cold water. Set aside.

Heat the oil in an oven-proof frying pan and add the garlic while it heats. When the oil begins to bubble gently and the garlic begins to colour slightly add the chilli flakes and continue to cook for 2 minutes. Remove the garlic from the oil and discard.

Add the passata and cream and bring to a gentle simmer. Stir through the spinach until wilted. Add the gnocchi and stir through to coat. Season with salt and add the fresh basil leaves.

Dot with blue cheese and ricotta and sprinkle generously with Parmesan. Sprinkle the top with a little water before placing in the oven to bake for 15 minutes.

Remove from the oven and allow to cool slightly before serving warm.

GOAT IN GOAT MILK TACOS

Mexicans have long prized a sweet treat of goat milk, known as cajeta. Here, our objective was to create a savoury cajeta to anoint the delicious, pull-apart simmered goat meat, a dish inspired by Alex Stupak, of New York's Empellón restaurants. This is a taco to dream about.

Serves 4

¼ cup beef dripping - you can also use pork fat or vegetable oil
1 small leg of goat, on the bone (available from select farms and butchers)
1 onion, sliced
1 litre goat milk

serving:
corn or flour tortillas
Mexican pickled chillies
lime wedges
shredded lettuce
finely sliced red onion

Melt the dripping in a large heavy pan, and brown the goat leg on all sides. Slip in the sliced onion, and colour in the fat. Pour over the goat milk and simmer the mixture, covered, for 3-5 hours. You need the meat to be able to pull away using just a fork.

Place the milk gravy into a sauce separator, to remove some, but not all, of the fat.

Strip the meat from the bone using two forks and place in a heatproof bowl.

To serve, rewarm the meat in the oven, and rewarm the gravy, which should be a delicious mixture of liquid and clusters of reduced goat milk. Pour some of the gravy over the meat, serve the rest in a gravy boat.

Serve family-style, each person making up their own tortilla using the ingredients suggested.

SUNDRIED TOMATO AND BASIL MASH

Slightly piquant, and freshened with the basil leaves, means that this mash is perfect with grilled meats. Make sure to make lots of the mash: leftovers make the most delicious potato cakes for breakfast, brunch or lunch.

Serves 4-6

900g potatoes, peeled
25g butter, plus extra for serving
1 clove garlic, minced
50-75ml cream
sea salt and fresh black pepper
1 cup sundried tomatoes (in oil, drained), julienned
half cup fresh basil leaves, julienned

Boil the potatoes in salted water until soft. Drain and dry over a low heat with the saucepan lid slightly ajar: this makes the potatoes fluffier.

Heat the butter, garlic and cream together in a saucepan. Mash the dry potatoes, then add the hot cream and butter to the potatoes and mash it all very well. Season with sea salt and pepper. Add the julienned sun-dried tomatoes and the basil, stirring gently, not mashing. Check seasoning. Serve with a knob of butter on top of the mash.

CLASSIC POTATO GRATIN

This is the simplest version of the classic potato gratin: lots of milk, no cheese, and not much work. Don't forget to rub the dish with the smashed garlic: it makes an enormous difference. A mandoline for slicing the potatoes will get things in the oven even faster.

Serves 4-6

750g potatoes, peeled
1 large clove garlic
salt and pepper
600ml milk
25g butter

Preheat the oven to 180°C.

Slice the potatoes with a sharp knife or, even better, a mandoline, which will give you even slices.

Smash the garlic clove with a knife and rub the smashed clove around the gratin dish. Let it become dry and tacky, then remove the bits. Butter the dish, using the butter wrapper. Layer the potato slices in circles, slightly overlapping, seasoning each layer with salt and pepper as you work.

Heat the milk just to boiling point, then pour over the potatoes so it comes up to the same level.

Dot with slices of cold butter and bake for 1 hour, to 75 minutes, until the top is browned, the interior fully cooked, and the milk completely absorbed.

POTATO STRAW CAKE

In addition to sounding totally fabulous, Desirée potatoes are perfect for potato straw cake, gifting you with that crunchy exterior that contrasts pleasingly with a creamy leek centre.

Serves 4

500g potatoes
sea salt and freshly ground black pepper
100g leeks
30g butter
30ml (2 tbsp) double cream
30ml (2 tbsp) olive oil

Heat the oven to 190°C.

Peel and grate the potatoes on the largest holes of a box grater, then place in a clean tea towel. Bundle up tightly in the towel, and squeeze out all the starchy liquid. Now, loosen the potato on the tea towel, and season with salt and pepper.

Slice the leeks and fry gently in approximately 10g of butter until softened, adding a tablespoon or two of water if necessary. When tender, add the double cream and reduce slightly. Cook for a further 5 minutes.

To assemble the cake, in a heavy, ovenproof frying pan, heat another 10g of butter and 1 tablespoon olive oil. Pack in half the potato mixture. Top with the creamed leeks, almost to the edge of the potato, then cover with the remaining potato.

Cook on the hob over a moderately high heat for 8 minutes so the bottom crisps. Invert the potato cake onto a plate – use a plate which is wider than the pan so that no butter juices course down your arms. Heat the remaining butter and olive oil in the pan, and then slide in the cake, so the crispy side is at the top.

Cook for another 10 minutes on the hob, then, to finish, place the whole pan in the hot oven for a final 10 minutes.

Serve in wedges.

SPLIT PEA & SPINACH DHAL WITH TADKA BUTTER

We have taken the traditional Indian technique of spiking a creamy dhal with a spice-rich tadka, but here we have made the spicy tadka into a flavoured butter, which you place on top of the finished dhal, and allow it to seep through the lush, starchy richness.

Serves 2-4

250g yellow split peas
5ml (1 tsp) ground turmeric
50g spinach leaves

tadka butter (see recipe on page 29)

naan bread and pickles, to serve

Rinse the split peas in several changes of water until the water runs clear – this makes a huge difference to the final texture of the dhal. Soak the split peas for 30 minutes in warm water, then drain and place in a pot with the turmeric. Cover with water, bring to the boil, then turn down the heat and simmer, covered, until it is almost cooked. Shred the spinach leaves, and just before the split peas are cooked, toss them into the mix just as the dhal is collapsing into velvety softness. Season to taste, scoop into a serving bowl, cut slices of the tadka butter and place on top of the hot dhal. Serve with naan bread and pickles.

CREAMED SPINACH

The steakhouse staple is a staple for a very good reason: weave slinky spinach through a slinky béchamel sauce, pepper it with crunchy breadcrumbs and give it a touch of spicy heat with freshly grated nutmeg, and you have an all-time classic.

Serves 2

20g butter
20g flour
200ml milk
nutmeg
salt and pepper
500g fresh spinach
handful breadcrumbs

Preheat the oven to 190°C.

Make a nutmeg béchamel: melt the butter in a pan, and stir in the flour to make a roux. Add the milk, constantly stirring as you do to avoid lumps. Cook over a medium heat, stirring regularly, until the mixture thickens and cooks. Grate in a generous amount of nutmeg, and season with salt and pepper.

Wash the spinach carefully to ensure any grit is removed, then place in a pan with just the water clinging to the leaves. Over medium heat, stir gently until the spinach wilts, and reduces dramatically in size. When all the leaves are wilted, strain off the spinach water – and reserve, this is a good tonic for the troops. Chop the leaves roughly, then stir into the béchamel. Spoon into an ovenproof dish and dot with breadcrumbs. Cook in the oven until the surface is browned and the béchamel is bubbling.

CORN CHEESE

Serves 2-4

50g butter, plus extra for topping
50g flour
500g milk
100g cheddar-style cheese, grated (we use Dubliner, Bandon Vale, Wexford Cheddar, or Irish local creamery cheese)
salt and pepper
5ml (1 tsp) grated nutmeg
450g frozen corn
3 bay leaves

If you should ever need to feed a gang of hungry adolescents speedily, then this will do the trick: they will be fighting over who gets to scrape the sticky, cheesy shards off the bowl. Once corn cheese is in your cooking repertoire, it will never leave, the mark of a true standard.

First make the cheese sauce. Melt the butter, and add the flour, stirring to make a roux. Slowly add the milk, stirring the whole time as you do. Cook on the hob for about 4 minutes, stirring very regularly so lumps don't form. Only at this point add most of the grated cheese (if you add at the beginning it will separate), leaving some for the topping. Season with salt, pepper and nutmeg.

Preheat the oven to 190°C.

Open the bag of corn (no need to defrost) and place in a large ovenproof dish. Slip in the three bay leaves. Pour over the cheese sauce and stir to combine. Dot with the rest of the grated cheese and thin slices of butter. Bake in the oven for 20 minutes, until the mixture is bubbling hot and the cheese topping is brown and crispy.

DILLISK, LEEK AND CHEESE TART

This recipe is inspired and informed by the great, influential tarts featured in various books by Deborah Madison, whose recipes in *The Greens Cookbook* remain a never-ending source of inspiration.

Serves 4-6

pastry:
160g plain flour
5ml (1 tsp) salt
60g butter
30ml (2 tbsp), plus 5ml (1 tsp), cold water

custard filling:
3 medium-sized leeks, sliced
50g butter
salt and black pepper
handful of dillisk
2 eggs
250ml cream
15ml (1 tbsp) mustard
100g Irish creamery cheese, grated (eg Wexford Cheddar, Bandon Vale, or Dubliner)

Put the flour and salt into a bowl. Cut the cold butter up into cubes, and rub into the flour with your fingertips. Add the cold water drop by drop, just until the mixture comes together in a ball. Cover with butter paper and refrigerate for an hour until chilled, then roll out and line a deep 20cm flan dish. Prick the base with a fork.

Place the butter paper on top of the pastry, and place in the freezer for another couple of hours until hard and frozen.

If you want to keep the pastry case for a longer time in the freezer, then wrap first to protect it.

When you are ready to make the tart, preheat the oven to 200°C. Part bake the pastry in the preheated oven for 20 minutes. There is no need to use baking beans if you have frozen the pastry. Take the pastry case out of the oven and prepare the filling.

Carefully wash the leeks and then sauté in the butter for approximately 5 minutes, until the leeks start to soften. Add about a quarter cup of water, and season with salt. Cover and cook for a further 5 minutes. Season again, this time with black pepper and a good handful of roughly chopped dilisk. Allow to cool slightly.

Beat the eggs in a bowl and stir in the cream, mustard and grated cheese. Fold in the cooled leeks.

Pour this custard into the part-cooked pastry shell and bake for approximately 20 minutes, or until the filling is just firm.

ANNE MARIE TOBIN — STUFFED RED & YELLOW PEPPERS

Before she became one of Ireland's best-known food stylists, Anne Marie Tobin was a hard-working chef in busy Dublin restaurants, her cooking characterised by a clean, fresh elegance. That's exactly what she gives us here, with a classic antipasto dish that never fails.

Serves 4

45ml (3 tbsp) olive oil
2 red peppers
2 yellow peppers
100g feta cheese, crumbled
35g toasted pine nuts
3 anchovies, finely chopped
1 tbsp capers, chopped
1 tbsp of flat leaf parsley, chopped
30g breadcrumbs
pinch of black pepper

Preheat oven to 170°C.

Drizzle one tablespoon of olive oil over the peppers and roast in the oven for 35-40 minutes. Remove from oven and stretch cling film over the roasting tray and allow to cool, this helps loosen the skin.

Peel the peppers, cut in half, remove seeds and trim into 8 rectangles.

In a separate bowl, mix all the remaining ingredients.

Place a tablespoon of the mixture on each pepper half and roll up.

Place on a serving platter and garnish with fresh basil. The peppers may be served hot or cold.

TOR-MEX

BUTTERMILK FLOUR TORTILLAS

Makes 10

280g plain flour
5ml (1 tsp) salt
50g butter, room temperature
125g buttermilk
75g water, boiling

The buttermilk gifts a pleasing piquancy.

Beat together the flour, salt and butter in a stand mixer with paddle attachment, until butter is just incorporated.

Measure the buttermilk in a jug, then add the measured boiling water to the buttermilk. Turn the mixer back on, and slowly add the warmed buttermilk, beating as you do. Beat for 3-4 minutes.

Using wet hands, take out the lump of dough, and rest it wrapped in baking paper and a cloth. Let it sit at room temperature for about 2 hours.

Divide the dough into 10 balls. Cover with a cloth. Roll each ball out, using a little flour to stop it sticking, and place on a piece of kitchen paper. Cover again with a damp cloth. Repeat with all the dough balls, stacking the rounds between pieces of kitchen paper. Leave to rest another half an hour.

Heat a heavy frying pan on the hob. The pan should be hot, but not blazing.

The final rolling can take place on a floured counter - work from the middle out, turning the tortilla as you roll and get it as thin as you can. You can also try rolling between two pieces of baking paper, or indeed use a Mexican tortilla press. Cook the tortillas in the hot pan, counting 20 seconds before turning. Turn again after another 20 seconds. The tortilla should fill with hot air pockets and start to puff up.

The tortilla is ready when it changes colour from an uncooked yellow dough, to a white tortilla. It takes about 2-3 minutes to cook each one. Don't overcook, or they will crisp up and not wrap properly. As they cook, wrap the tortillas snugly in a tea towel. This will help them to steam and soften.

PATRICK RYAN — BATCH LOAF

'In order to make a batch loaf you can't simply bake just one. You literally have to bake a batch of them' writes Patrick Ryan of Firehouse Bakery. 'Each loaf sits side by side, which prevents the crust forming on the sides, which keeps the loaf really soft.' The buttermilk gives the bread an added richness.

Makes 4 loaves

1kg strong white flour
20g salt
20g fresh yeast, of if you only have dried yeast, use 1 sachet or 7g
700g buttermilk

23cm square baking tin

Mix the flour and salt in a clean bowl. Crumble the yeast into the flour. Add the buttermilk to the flour and mix.

Bring the dough together with your hands or with a spatula. Turn the dough out onto a lightly floured surface and knead for approximately 10 minutes, until the dough is soft and very elastic.

Place the dough in an oiled bowl, cover with a damp tea towel or wrap in cling film and leave to prove for 90 minutes. Turn the proved dough out and knock it back. Divide the dough into 4 equal portions, approximately 450g each. Shape each portion of dough into a rough round and leave them to rest on the counter for 10 minutes. We call this the bench rest. This allows the gluten to relax before final shaping. Once the dough has rested, roll each portion of dough into a tight round and place in your baking tray, allowing each portion of dough to just touch each other. Cover and allow to prove again for about 60 to 90 minutes. Just before baking, the dough should be well risen with a nice bounce to the dough when touched. There should be no fear of the dough collapsing when touched.

Preheat the oven to 220°C. Place a roasting tray into the base of the oven. When ready to bake, place the loaves into the oven and pour boiling water into the hot roasting tray, which should release a blast of steam during cooking. Bake the loaves for about 35-40 minutes.

JAPANESE MILK BREAD

This recipe is adapted from one that appears on the website of The Real Bread Campaign — sustainweb.org. The recipe was originally for burger buns, created by baker David Wright, and it uses the Japanese technique of tangzhong, where a roux is made first, and added to the dough, which will gelatinise the starch, lock in moisture and make for an incredibly light, white and fluffy bread.

tangzhong:
80g milk
80g water
30g white bread flour

dough:
500g strong white flour
105g buttermilk
105g water
1 egg
40g olive oil
30g fresh yeast
30g sugar
10g milk powder
10g salt

olive oil
double cream to glaze

First make the tangzhong by whisking together the milk, water and flour in a small saucepan over moderate heat, and stirring continuously until the mixture thickens and becomes glossy, about 4-5 minutes. Allow to cool.

Place the dough ingredients into a stand mixer and beat together, using a dough hook, until combined. Leave for 15 minutes to rest (covered in the bowl), then add the tangzhong and beat at moderate speed until the dough forms, and starts to pull away from the sides of the bowl (about 7 minutes).

Oil an airtight container that will fit double the amount of the dough, and place the dough inside. Leave for just over an hour while the dough rises to double its size.

Divide the dough into eight, and form eight balls of dough. Place into a round loaf tin, with one dough ball in the middle, and seven surrounding it. Cover with a cloth, or let sit in an airtight container. Let the dough rise for approximately an hour, or until the dough spreads, and reaches the top of the tin, and then bake in an oven which has been preheated to 200°C. Check after 30 minutes. The bread is ready when it sounds hollow when tapped on the base, or reaches over 90°C.

KHACHAPURI

300g plain flour
170g butter
2.5ml (½ tsp) salt
2 eggs (plus 2 eggs for serving – optional)
60ml natural yogurt
150g cottage cheese
1 x 125g ball Mozzarella
150g Feta cheese

23cm square baking tin

If you want to make the bread into traditional boat shapes, then, divide the dough in four. Roll out each quarter into a circle and, using your fingers, roll in two opposite sides of the circle, with pinching and pressing movements to create a canoe shape. Twist the ends of the dough. Fill each boat with a quarter of the cheese mixture and bake for 50 minutes. Just before serving, break an egg into the bread, and cook for three minutes to set.

'If any equivalent to fast food exists in Georgia, it must be khachapuri. Although Georgians are not accustomed to eating out frequently, even the smallest towns have hole-in-the-wall cafes where piping hot khachapuri may be consumed on the spot or taken out', writes American author Darra Goldstein, in her book *The Georgian Feast*. While khachapuri is described as a 'bread', the dough can be yeasty, flaky or cakelike. This one, adapted from Darra's book, is a rich, flaky pastry version, with yogurt used to tenderise the dough. Perfect picnic food, a great take out.

Measure the flour into a large bowl, and mix in the butter until the mixture resembles breadcrumbs. Stir in the salt. Make a well in the centre of the flour, break in 1 egg, add the yogurt, and beat with a fork before folding into the flour mixture to form a dough. Wrap the dough and chill for 1 hour in the fridge.

Preheat the oven to 190°C.

Grate the cheese, and tear up any bits that are too soft and bendy to go through the grater. Combine all the cheeses with 3 tbsp (45ml) water.

Oil the baking tin. Take the dough out of the fridge and place on a lightly floured surface. Divide the dough in half. Roll out the first half to fit the square baking tin. Press the dough lightly into the tin. Cover with the grated cheese, going almost, but not quite to the edges. Roll out the second half of dough, and place on top of the cheese. Seal the edges of the tart, beat the second egg, and use to brush the tart all over. Prick with a fork in two or three places in the middle.

Bake in the oven for 50 minutes, until just brown. Serve warm, cut into squares or finger lengths.

DERVLA JAMES — CRANBERRY & BLOOD ORANGE SCONES

Dervla James, of Sligo's Pudding Row, is one of Ireland's most admired bakers, blessed with a Midas touch when it comes to conjuring the lightest, zestiest scones imaginable.

Makes 8-10

450g plain flour
10ml (2 tsp) baking powder
pinch of sea salt
40g vanilla sugar
90g very cold butter
zest of 2 blood oranges
90g dried cranberries
190ml full fat milk
2 large eggs

Preheat the oven to 195°C.

Sift your flour, baking powder and salt into a large bowl. I like to have plenty of room to gently but effectively mix the dough.

Add sugar and chop the chilled butter into the dry ingredients. Work quickly in order not to melt the butter. Rub between your fingers to create the texture of tiny, golden buttery breadcrumbs.

Add orange zest and cranberries to the bowl and mix well throughout the dry ingredients. Make a well in the centre, whisk the milk and eggs together vigorously in a jug, and add two thirds of the liquids to the bowl. Using your hand like a wide paddle, simply bring the dough together and gradually apply pressure and push it together into a soft ball, not too tight. Add the remaining liquid if required, leaving a little liquid for brushing scones before baking.

Toss onto a floured surface and gently knead, flatten out and cut with your desired cutter - frilly, flat, whatever you fancy. Place onto a baking sheet lined with baking paper if you have some. These sheets are reusable - waste not, want not.

Brush tops with a little of the eggy milk mixture that's leftover and bake for 14-16 minutes. Remove and leave to cool, if you can wait that long.

We highly recommend you top with cream and your favourite seasonal compote.

SEAWEED CRACKERS

A pasta machine is great for making crackers, and it's also great fun to use. But if you don't have one, then use a rolling pin, and roll the dough as thin as you possibly can. This recipe was inspired by Bridget Healy.

Makes approx 30

230g plain or spelt flour
20g rye flour
40g butter
5ml (1 tsp) sugar
2.5ml (½ tsp) salt
150ml milk
1 cup finely ground seaweed
sesame seeds / fennel seeds (optional)

Measure the flours into the bowl, and rub in the butter until it resembles fine breadcrumbs. Mix in the sugar and salt. Add the milk and gather the mixture into a dough, with your hands. Knead the dough lightly, and then put it in the fridge to rest for 2 hours.

Lightly grease a baking tray and heat the oven to 180°C. Flour a large workspace.

Cut the dough into 6 equal-sized pieces. Take one piece, and cover the remaining dough pieces with a damp cloth while you work.

Press lightly on the piece of dough. Sprinkle on the seaweed and seeds and press again. Examples of combinations might be kelp and fennel, or dried seaweed salad with sesame seeds.

Put dough through a pasta machine on the widest setting.

Lightly press in some more seeds or seaweed and roll again. Continue until the second last setting on the machine.

Cut into approximate squares or rectangles, and place each cracker onto the baking tray, using a spatula to lift the delicate pieces.

Bake in the oven for approximately 10 minutes, until light brown.

Cool on a wire tray and store in an airtight container.

ICE CREAM SANDWICH COOKIES

Sandwiching ice cream between cookies is a fab, messy treat: you might need to eat this whilst standing over the kitchen sink. We use this recipe – a very old and still wonderful recipe for peanut biscuits from Sally's mother, Margie – to make the two sides of the sandwich. The cookies are slightly chewy, crispy, salty, with a lacy light texture that sandwiches your favourite ice cream to perfection.

Makes approx 20

115g butter
225g caster sugar
1 egg
15ml (1 tbsp) golden syrup
150g plain flour
10ml (2 tsp) cocoa powder
10ml (2 tsp) baking powder
pinch of salt
150g salted peanuts

Your favourite flavour of ice cream.

Heat the oven to 180°C. Line a baking sheet with baking paper.

Cream together the butter and the sugar until pale. Beat in the egg, and add the golden syrup. Sift together the flour, cocoa, baking powder and salt, and fold into the butter mix. Fold in the peanuts.

Take heaped teaspoonfuls of the mixture and place on the baking tray, leaving plenty of room for the cookies to spread. You will probably have to do two or three bakes. Bake in the preheated oven for 10-12 minutes. When you take the cookies out of the oven, they will be very soft, but a few minutes on a cooling rack will crisp them up.

Take the ice cream out of the freezer for about 15 minutes before using. Spoon onto a cookie and top with a second cookie. Put back in the deep freeze for a few minutes to firm up again.

CARRAGEEN PUDDING WITH PEACH MELBA

Auguste Escoffier's timeless dessert was his homage to the great Australian soprano, Nellie Melba. We have simply added our homage to carrageen, Ireland's luscious seaweed dessert. Together, the pair are pitch perfect.

Serves 4

carrageen pudding:

1 fistful of dried carrageen
900ml full-cream milk
1 vanilla pod
1 free range egg
15ml (1 tbsp) caster sugar

peach melba:

4 peaches
1 cup sugar
2 cups water
5ml (1 tsp) vanilla essence
250g raspberries
15ml (1 tbsp) peach cooking water
juice of ½ a lemon

To make the pudding: soak the carrageen in water for 10 minutes, then squeeze it in your fist to remove the water and add it to the milk with the vanilla pod. Bring very slowly to the boil, and keep on a low simmer for 20 minutes. Strain the milk, pressing the jelly that collects around the fronds, as well as any escaping vanilla seeds.

Slice the vanilla pod down the centre and remove the seeds along with the liquid. Add this to the strained milk.

Separate the egg and beat the yolk with the sugar. Slowly add the milk to the beaten yolk. Pour into a bowl. Now, beat the egg white until stiff and fluffy. Add this to the milk too. Leave the pudding in the fridge until set.

To make the peach melba: cut the peaches in half, lengthways and twist slightly giving you two halves. No need to remove the stone yet. Dissolve the sugar in the water in a pan, and bring to the boil. Add the vanilla essence. Place the peach halves in the water, turn the heat down and simmer for about 5 minutes, turning the peaches over about half way.

Purée the raspberries with 1 tablespoon of the cooking water from the peaches. Add the juice of half a lemon, and sieve to remove raspberry pips.

Remove the peaches from the sauce, stone and skin. Serve with the raspberry purée and carrageen pudding.

GRAINNE O'KEEFFE — VANILLA PANNA COTTA WITH STRAWBERRIES

This is the sort of boom-boom-boom cooking that has established Grainne O'Keeffe, of Dublin's Clanbrassil House, as one of the most admired chefs of her generation. It's hit after hit after hit of sheer deliciousness.

Serves 6

panna cotta:
3 gelatine leaves
450ml double cream
200ml whole milk
100g white caster sugar
1 vanilla pod

honey tuile:
55g butter
115g honey
25g muscovado sugar
16g plain flour

macerated strawberries:
400g Irish strawberries
50g white caster sugar

To make the panna cotta, soak the gelatine in cold water. Bring cream, milk, sugar and vanilla to 98°C. Add gelatine and whisk. Pass through a sieve. Spoon into moulds, or glasses, and refrigerate.

To make the tuiles: bring the butter, honey and muscovado to the boil in a pan. Sift in the flour. Refrigerate for 1 hour. Preheat oven to 175°C. Line a baking tray with a silicone liner. Using a palette knife, spread circles of the tuile mix on the liner. Bake for 9 minutes. Allow to cool and store in an airtight container, separated by greaseproof paper.

Cut strawberries into quarters, mix with the sugar and leave for 2 hours until the juices start to come out and the sugar is dissolved.

GRAINNE MULLINS – BLACKCURRANT LEAF PANNA COTTA

The refined rusticity of this recipe demonstrates exactly why Grainne Mullins was garlanded as Euro-Toques Young Chef of the Year. Grainne uses blackcurrant leaf but advises that you should 'feel free to be adventurous: vanilla is always a good call but the likes of lavender, fennel seeds, or even rosemary can be a fun way to explore new flavours.'

Serves 4

panna cotta:
5 gelatine leaves
355ml milk
355ml cream
100g caster sugar
20g blackcurrant leaf

blackcurrant jelly:
2½ gelatine leaves
250g blackcurrant purée
100g caster sugar
25g lemon juice

For the panna cotta: soak the gelatine in cold water. Place the milk, cream and caster sugar into a saucepan and bring to the boil. Remove from the heat and add the blackcurrant leaf. Leave to infuse for 15 minutes. Sieve the mixture. Squeeze excess water from the gelatine and whisk into the mixture. Pour into prepared glasses. Allow to set in the fridge for 3 hours.

For the jelly: soak the gelatine in cold water. Heat the purée and sugar in a pan until the sugar dissolves. Squeeze excess water from the gelatine and whisk into the purée. Add the lemon juice. Using a jug, pour jelly over the set panna cotta. Allow to cool in the fridge for a further 1 hour.

VANESSA MURPHY — ARROZ CON LECHE

Asturias, in north western Spain, claims to be the home of rice pudding. In Dublin, the home of Spanish rice pudding is Vanessa and Anna's Las tapas de Lola, one of the city's best-loved places to eat. This darling dish of rice pudding is typical of their lyrical, gutsy style of cooking.

Serves 10

2 litres whole fat milk
250g caster sugar
280g short grain rice
rind of 1 lemon
2 cinnamon sticks
ground cinnamon to sprinkle on top

In a thick-bottomed pan, cook all the ingredients, apart from the ground cinnamon, on a low heat for 1½ hours. Don't boil.

Once cooked, remove the cinnamon sticks and lemon rind.

Serve cold with a sprinkling of ground cinnamon on top; the amount depends on how much you love cinnamon.

DARREN HOGARTY — RICE PUDDING WITH WHISKEY SAUCE

Darren Hogarty takes simple things, and makes them super-special. Here is the chef's utterly singular take on rice pudding, the nursery staple rocketed into the stratosphere.

Serves 8

225g short grain rice
1 litre milk, plus 200ml
100g caster sugar
50g butter
8 egg yolks
300ml double cream
150g crème fraîche

whiskey sauce:
450g caster sugar
180ml water
500ml double cream
100ml Irish whiskey
5ml (1 tsp) sea salt

Place the rice in cold water to cover and then bring to the boil, drain and refresh. Boil 1 litre of the milk, half the sugar and all the butter in a large pan with the rice. Once it reaches boiling point, turn down to a simmer. Cook for 8-10 minutes or until the rice is tender.

Beat the egg yolks and remaining caster sugar together in a bowl. Boil the cream with the remaining 200ml milk and pour onto the yolks, whisking until pale and creamy. Stir the mixture gradually into the pan containing the rice and cook on a low heat. Once it is suitably thick, take off the heat, stir in the crème fraîche and leave in the fridge to cool.

Whiskey sauce: heat sugar and water in a medium, clean, saucepan over a medium heat, for 2–3 minutes. The sugar will melt and small bubbles will start appearing. Don't be tempted to stir, this can encourage the caramel to crystallize – just swirl it round using the handle.

Once the sugar has started boiling, after about 5 minutes, it should be light brown in colour. Continue boiling until it has become medium brown in colour. Remove the saucepan from the heat and pour the cream into the mixture. It will hiss and spit and seem to solidify but be patient and return to the heat for 2–3 minutes, then add whiskey. Stir through the salt and transfer to a glass jar or bowl and let cool to room temperature or pop in the fridge for 20 minutes.

To serve, spoon the rice pudding into glasses or bowls. Pour on whiskey caramel sauce and swirl.

TRISH MESSOM – PORTUGUESE CUSTARD TARTS

Trish Messom, of Bantry's The Stuffed Olive, is one of those great cooks who manage to make even complicated things seem simple and logical. That's exactly what she does here with her riff on pasteis de nata – Portugese custard tarts. The recipe appeared originally in *The Stuffed Olive Cookbook*.

Makes 12

3 large egg yolks
125g caster sugar
30g cornflour
5ml (1 tsp) vanilla essence, or 1 vanilla pod split, seeds scraped out
175ml full-fat milk
225ml double cream
butter, for greasing
300g ready-rolled puff pastry
plain flour, for dusting
icing sugar, for dusting

In a bowl, mix the egg yolks, sugar, cornflour and vanilla. Boil the milk and cream together in a saucepan. Add the milk and cream in a thin stream to the eggs and sugar, mix until well combined. Return the custard to a clean saucepan over a low to medium heat, stirring continuously until it comes to the boil and thickens. Remove from the heat and transfer to a clean bowl and cover the surface with cling film to prevent a skin from forming. Cool.

Preheat the oven to 180°C.

Grease the wells of a 12-hole muffin tray with butter. Lay the puff pastry onto a clean work surface lightly dusted with flour and icing sugar. Cut the pastry in half and place one sheet on top of the other. Roll the pastry sheets up like a Swiss roll, and cut the roll into twelve slices. Lay each of the rolled pastry slices flat onto the work surface, and roll out into 10cm discs using a rolling pin.

Press a pastry disc into each of the wells of the prepared muffin tray and divide the cooled custard equally among the pastry cases.

Transfer the muffin tray to the oven and bake the tarts for 18-20 minutes or until the custard has set and is pale golden brown and the pastry is crisp and golden brown. Allow to cool in the tin before dusting with icing sugar.

OREO MILLIONAIRES

Who wants to eat an Oreo millionaire? You do. This pure shazam of caramel, chocolate and biscuit hits every pleasure part of your senses: boom!

MAKES APPROX 20

2 packets chocolate Oreo biscuits
120g butter, melted

caramel layer:
150g butter
45ml (3 tbsp) caster sugar
60ml (4 tbsp) golden syrup
1 can (397ml) condensed milk

200g dark chocolate

23cm square baking tin

First make the base. Grind the Oreos in a food processor, and mix the crumbled biscuits with the melted butter. Press into the tin and leave to cool and set completely (about half an hour).

Make the caramel by melting the butter, sugar, syrup and milk in a saucepan, stirring continuously. Increase the heat and cook, stirring all the time, for about 15 minutes. The sauce will darken and thicken as it comes together. Spread the caramel over the Oreo base. Leave to chill in the fridge.

Melt the chocolate in a bowl, set over a pan of boiling water. Once melted, pour over the caramel. Leave in the fridge until the chocolate hardens. Use a sharp knife to cut into squares.

GRAHAM HERTERICH – MILK CEREAL CUPCAKES

Graham Herterich, also known as The Cupcake Bloke, is a prodigiously original baker, able to take a simple idea and transport it to another universe of flavour. Milk cereal cupcakes! Who knew?

Makes 12

For the cereal milk:
40g breakfast cereal of your choice, eg Crunchy Nut Cornflakes - cereals that absorb a lot of milk, such as Weetabix, are not suitable
60g milk

cupcakes:
165g butter, softened at room temperature
165g caster sugar
3 eggs, lightly beaten
½ of the softened cereal
165g self-raising flour
½ of the cereal milk
additional cereal for topping and decoration

buttercream frosting:
150g butter, softened at room temperature
300g icing sugar
remainder of cereal milk
remainder of softened cereal

Start by making the cereal milk by simply pouring the milk over the cereal and leaving to soak for half an hour. Strain the cereal and keep both the milk and the softened cereal.

Preheat the oven to 180°C and line a 12-hole muffin tin with paper cases.

To make the cupcakes: cream the butter and sugar together in a bowl until pale. Beat in the eggs one at a time and stir in half of the softened cereal.

Fold in the flour using a large metal spoon, adding a little of the cereal milk until the mixture has a dropping consistency. Spoon the mixture into the paper cases until they are half full and top with some crushed cereal of choice.

Bake in the oven for 15-18 minutes, or until golden-brown on top and a skewer inserted into one of the cakes comes out clean. Allow to cool for 10 minutes, then remove from the muffin tin and cool on a wire rack.

For the buttercream frosting: beat the butter in a large bowl until soft. Add half the icing sugar and beat until smooth.

Then add the remaining icing sugar, the softened cereal and one tbsp of cereal milk adding more milk if necessary, until the mixture is smooth and creamy.

Spoon the icing into a piping bag with a star nozzle, and pipe the icing using a spiralling motion onto the cupcakes in a large swirl. Gently dip the cupcake into more of the cereal.

Enjoy with a large glass of milk!

MARK JENNINGS — ELDERFLOWER AND STRAWBERRY CUSTARD TART

'Custard tart sounds simple, yet it's both decadent and comforting and just not to be underrated,' says Mark Jennings of West Cork's iconic Pilgrims Restaurant.

Serves 12

elderflower custard:
200g elderflowers, picked, tough stems removed
1 litre cream
18 egg yolks
300g caster sugar

sweet pastry:
250g plain flour
125g unsalted butter
100g icing sugar
1 large egg

28-30cm loose bottomed tart tin
fresh elderflowers, strawberries and elder flower cordial to decorate

Day 1: pick elderflowers on a dry sunny morning. When you get back to the kitchen scald your cream in a pan, when it just comes to the boil pour it over the fresh and fragrant elderflowers. Allow to steep and cool in the bowl. Pop into the fridge until the next day.

Place the butter, cut into 2cm cubes, into a food processor with the sugar. Pulse, then turn the machine on full. When butter and sugar are fully blended add the egg. Pulse until smooth, then add half the flour, process for 5-10 seconds and repeat with the remaining flour. Stop as soon as the mixture comes together.

On a clean dry surface tip the contents of the bowl out, quickly push the mixture together into one lump. Wrap the dough in cling film and chill in the fridge overnight.

Day 2: Roll out pastry shell until 3-4mm thick. Press into greased tin. Chill for at least one hour.

Preheat the oven to 180°C. Cover the pastry with a sheet of baking paper and beans, bake blind for 10 minutes. Turn oven down to 120°C. In a mixing bowl, whisk egg yolks and caster sugar until dissolved. Strain elderflower cream and heat in a pan. Pour onto egg yolks and sugar, whisk until combined then pour into jug. Place the tart shell back in the oven and pour elderflower custard mixture right to the brim.

Bake for 20 minutes until the custard appears to be just set but not firm. Allow to cool to room temperature before decorating with strawberries that have been tossed in a little elderflower cordial and sprinkle some more freshly picked elderflowers on top.

ADRIAN MARTIN – CHOCOLATE AND HAZELNUT TART

Adrian Martin says that this tart – also known as death by chocolate – 'always reminds me of Ferrero Rocher. I love a tart where you can surprise people with the different flavours in the mixture.' The chef is really spoiling us.

Serves 6-8

chocolate tuiles:

2 egg whites
90g caster sugar
55g plain flour
5ml (1 tsp) cocoa powder
55g unsalted butter, melted and cooled

320g shortcrust pastry

chocolate tart:

50g toasted hazelnuts
450g dark chocolate, broken into pieces
5ml (1 tsp) cocoa powder
4 eggs
85g caster sugar
230ml cream
120ml milk

chocolate and hazelnut ice cream, to serve

For the tuiles: line a baking tray with a silicone liner. Preheat the oven to 175°C. Put the egg whites and sugar in a bowl and lightly beat with a fork. Sift in the flour with the cocoa powder and stir to mix well. Add the butter and stir until evenly blended. Using a palette knife, spread a few thin strips of the tuile mix on the liner. Bake for 7–8 minutes until they are brown around the edges with a matt appearance. Leave to cool for a minute or two. While they are still pliable, lift each tuile with a palette knife and twist to resemble a pair of wings. Leave to cool and set. They will become crisp and brittle. Use all the mixture to make extras as these break really easily. The mixture normally makes 10–15. Store in an airtight container until ready to serve.

Preheat the oven to 180ºC.

Roll out the pastry and line six mini loose-bottomed tart tins, then line the pastry with some scrunched up baking paper or heatproof cling film. Fill with either baking beans, rice or dried marrowfat peas. Bake the pastry blind for 10 minutes, then remove from the oven and whatever you used to line it during blind baking. Return the tartlet tins to the oven and bake the pastry for a further 5–10 minutes in the oven until crispy. Take out and allow to cool.

Lower oven temperature to 90°C.

For the chocolate filling, start by pulsing the hazelnuts in a food processor until they are coarsely chopped. Place the chocolate, cocoa powder, eggs and sugar in a bowl. Boil the cream and milk together. Pour the hot milk-cream mix over the chocolate mix and whisk until smooth, then pass through a sieve. Once sieved, stir in the hazelnuts. Pour this mixture into the pastry cases and bake at 90°C for 30–40 minutes, or until there's a slight wobble in the centre. Leave to cool, then place in the fridge until ready to serve.

Serve each individual tart on a plate and top with a tuile. To finish, add a neat scoop of chocolate and hazelnut ice cream on the side.

LILLY HIGGINS – MILK TART

'Milk tart is a traditional South African dessert that we used to always have at barbecues and get-togethers in Zimbabwe when we were small,' says *Irish Times* food writer Lilly Higgins. 'Someone always brought shortbread and there was always milk tart.' Lilly advises to 'try to make your pastry very thin, as this tart is all about lightness to give a crisp, buttery case with the smooth vanilla filling.'

Serves 10-12

1 litre milk
15ml (1 tbsp) butter
2 eggs
150g sugar
45ml (3 tbsp) cornflour
45ml (3 tbsp) plain flour
15ml (l tbsp) vanilla essence
1 blind-baked pastry case (I add 5ml (1 tsp) cinnamon to my own homemade butter pastry)
ground cinnamon, to decorate

Bring the milk and butter to the boil in a medium saucepan. Really keep an eye on it, as the milk will boil over the second you look away!

Cream the eggs, sugar, cornflour, flour and vanilla essence together in a bowl. Add some of the hot milk to the egg mixture, then pour it all back into the pan. Heat for 5-10 minutes, stirring until the mixture thickens. Keep stirring and don't allow the mixture to boil.

Pour into the pastry case. Leave to cool and set, then sprinkle generously with cinnamon before serving.

MARK MORIARTY –
CHURROS WITH MILK JAM

Mark Moriarty won the San Pellegrino World Young Chef of the Year award, and this inspiring dish of churros with milk jam shows the technical mastery, and the effervescent creativity, that is the signature of everything he cooks.

Serves 8

milk jam:
1 litre Irish milk
250g sugar
5ml (1 tsp) bicarbonate of soda

the churros:
80g butter, chopped
250ml water
150g plain flour
15ml (1 tbsp) caster sugar
2 medium eggs, beaten
vegetable oil, to deep-fry
icing sugar, for dusting

To make the milk jam: add the ingredients to a pan and cook over a medium heat for 2-2½ hours until it is brown and jam like. You can add glass marbles to the pan to stop it sticking to the bottom, otherwise stir every few minutes.

To make the churros: melt the butter and water together in a pan, add the flour and sugar, and cook over a medium heat for 2 minutes, mixing all the time.

Transfer to a mixer with a paddle, and begin mixing, adding the eggs until the dough is glossy and smooth. Transfer to a piping bag with a star nozzle and reserve.

Heat the oil to 180°C in the deep fat fryer. Pipe the dough into the oil using scissors to cut to length – they should be 3cm long.

Fry until golden in colour, remove and dust in icing sugar. Serve churros with the warmed milk jam dipping sauce.

CAITLIN RUTH — BURNT MILK & WHISKEY COCKTAIL

This is Caitlin Ruth's Irish version of an espresso martini, a drink where every ingredient is discernible, but none overpowers. The cocktail, once shaken, will be foamy and fluffy enough to let you sit a couple of coffee beans on top for decoration, if you're feeling fancy. And you will certainly feel pretty fancy after one of these.

Serves 2-3

burnt milk mix:
500ml milk
4 cardamom pods, just cracked
6 black peppercorns
5 cloves
½ star anise
thumb of ginger root, sliced

70ml local honey
a pinch of sea salt

to assemble cocktail:
100ml Irish whiskey
100ml strong espresso
100ml burnt milk mix

Place the milk, cardamom pods, peppercorns, cloves, anise and ginger into a small pan on lowest possible heat and simmer until liquid is reduced to 150ml approximately. We call this 'burnt milk', but actually the bottom of your pan shouldn't actually be burnt, but a deep golden brown. This gives the distinctive flavour to the milk.

Strain out the spices and discard. Stir the honey and sea salt into the milk. This stage can be done ahead of time, and the burnt, spiced, sweetened milk kept in the fridge for a few days.

Shake ingredients together in a cocktail shaker or jar, full to the brim with ice. Shake for longer than you think you should, then strain evenly into 2 or 3 glasses. You will have some milk mix left over for another time. Like now.

BRANDY ALEXANDER

SERVES 1

45ml brandy
30ml creme de cacao
30ml cream
nutmeg

Brandy Alexander brings out the poet in people. 'As toothsome as candy, but as seductive as surreptitious liquor', wrote the late Michael Jackson, who suggested you think of it as 'An extravagant cocktail for an afternoon rendezvous.' Of course, Leslie Feist said it all when she sang that Brandy Alexander 'Goes down easy/It goes down easy.' Feist also cautioned: 'I'm his Brandy Alexander/Always get him into trouble.' Trouble coming.

Mix the first three ingredients together in a cocktail shaker filled with lots of ice, then strain into a chilled, stemmed cocktail glass. A little dusting of nutmeg on top and you're good.

WHITE RUSSIAN

SERVES 1

50ml vodka
30ml kahlúa
30ml cream

Allegedly invented in the Hotel Metropole in Brussels, in 1949, the White Russian came back into focus when it featured in the Coen brothers' cult movie, *The Big Lebowski.* Jeff 'The Dude' Lebowski's favourite cocktail is a White Russian, which he is partial to drinking at pretty much anytime of the day: 'Hey, careful, man, there's a beverage here!'

Stir the ingredients together, then pour over a rubble of ice cubes in a glass. To make the Dude's favourite even funkier, swap out the cream for Caitlin Ruth's burnt cream (see previous page).

BANANA & CORNFLAKE MILK SHAKE

This recipe is built around the funky idea of cereal milk™, invented (and trademarked) by Christina Tosi of Momofuku Milk Bar. Christina recognised that the best bit about eating a bowl of cereal is the milk left at the bottom of the bowl. She bottled and sold the cereal-flavoured milk, and it was an instant success, spawning many malty milky recipes ever since. As many of us share a childhood love of cornflakes and banana, this Banana Cornflake Milkshake is an homage to Christina Tosi for such a great idea.

Serves 4

100g cornflakes
700ml milk
30g light brown sugar
2 scoops vanilla ice cream
2 bananas, sliced
100ml double cream
2.5ml (½ tsp) cinnamon
dried banana chips and cereal flakes to decorate

Heat the oven to 170°C. Place the cornflakes on a baking tray and bake in the preheated oven for 10 minutes. Allow to cool briefly.

Pour the milk into a large 2-litre jug, and add the cooled cornflakes – reserving a small amount to garnish the glasses. Leave to steep for half an hour at room temperature.

Strain the mixture, pushing all the cornflakes against the strainer. Place the milk in the fridge for an hour to chill completely. Discard, or compost the soaked flakes.

To assemble the shake, place the milk, sugar, ice cream, sliced bananas, cream and cinnamon into a blender and blend until smooth.

Pour into four tall glasses and decorate with banana chips and cereal flakes and a colourful paper straw.

BUTTERMILK LEMONADE

Milk is more hydrating even than water. That's why these cool milk-based drinks are perfect for a hot day.

juice of 1 lemon
15ml (1 tbsp) caster sugar
500ml buttermilk

Combine the lemon juice and sugar, stirring until the sugar is dissolved. Pour in the buttermilk, whisking, so everything is smoothly combined.

SALTED MINT LASSI

5ml (1 tsp) cumin seeds
450g natural yogurt
20ml water
10 mint leaves, plus extra to decorate
5ml (1 tsp) salt
ice cubes

In a small pan over medium heat, toast the cumin seeds until they are fragrant, then grind to a fine powder. In a blender, place yogurt, water and mint and process until the mint is chopped. Add the ground cumin, the salt and the ice cubes, and process. Pour the frothy, ice-laden lassi into tall glasses, and top with some extra mint leaves.

SWEET MANGO LASSI

2 very ripe mangoes, peeled and stoned
450g natural yogurt
sprinkle of ground cardamom
ice cubes
honey, to taste

In a blender, process the mango flesh and any juices, yogurt, cardamom, ice cubes and honey until the drink is smooth. If it is too thick, add a little cold water so it pours freely.

BEETROOT KVASS

3 beetroots, raw, peeled
15ml (1 tbsp) salt
25ml whey (leftover liquid after you have made labneh, for example)
fresh water

Chop the beets roughly, then place in a large glass jug with the salt and whey. Top up the glass jug with fresh water, and cover. Keep it in your kitchen at room temperature for 2-3 days, then chill in the fridge before serving, using a tea strainer or sieve. When you have drunk most of the kvass, you can top up the water and you will get a second run of the drink, less powerful, but still good.

INDEX

A

Ancho Chilli & Lime Butter 29
Arroz Con Leche 115
Asian Dipping Sauce 50

B

Baked Gnocchi 80
Baked Plaice with Cherry Tomatoes 62
Batch Loaf 98
Béarnaise Sauce 37
Béchamel Sauce 41, 61
Beetroot Kvass 137
Blue Cheese & Sage Butter 29
Bolognaise Sauce 76
Brandy Alexander 134
Bread Sauce 41
Brown Butter 26
Burnt Milk & Whiskey Cocktail 132
Butter 26, 28
Buttermilk French Toast 48
Buttermilk Lemonade 137

C

Caesar Dressing 39
Carrageen Pudding 110
Chicken Empanadas 75
Chicken Liver Pâté 52
Chicken, Ricotta-stuffed Spatchcocked 72
Chocolate & Hazelnut Tart 127
Churros 130
Clarified Butter 26
Cocktails 132, 134
Compound Butter 28
Corn Cheese 90
Cottage Cheese 34
Cottage Cheesecake 34
Crab Cakes 60
Crackers, Seaweed 106
Crème Fraîche 41
Cupcakes, Milk Cereal 122
Custard Tart, Elderflower & Strawberry 124

D

Dalton, Jacinta 32
Davidson, Tony 68
Dede, Ahmet 30
Dhal 88

E

Empanadas 75

F

Feta Dip 50
Finnan Haddie 58
Flavoured Butters 28
Flower Butter 29
Fox, Niamh 54
French Toast 48

G

Garlic and Parsley Butter 29
Georgian Cheese Bread 102
Gnocchi 80
Goat In Goat Milk Tacos 81
Gremolata Butter 29

H

Haddock Goujons 68
Hake and Prawns in Saffron Béchamel 61
Herb Butter 29
Herterich, Graham 122
Higgins, Lilly 128
Hogarty, Darren 116
Hollandaise Sauce 37

I

Ice Cream Sandwich Cookies 108
Irish Cacio e Pepe Butter 29

J

Jambon 54
James, Dervla 105
Japanese Milk Bread 100
Jennings, Mark 124

K

Kai Labneh 32
Kefir 39
Khachapuri 102
Kidneys with Juniper 79
Kvass 37, 137

L

Labneh 32
Labneh Pearls 32
Lassi 137
Lassi 137
Leek, Dillisk & Cheese Tart 93

M

Mango Lassi 137
Martin, Adrian 127
Mash, Sundried Tomato and Basil 82

INDEX

McDermott, Brian 37, 49
McKenna, Clodagh 52
McMahon, Aran 39
Messom, Trish 119
Milk Jam 130
Milk Mojo 75
Milk Shake, Banana and Cornflake 136
Milk Tart 128
Mint Lassi 137
Miyazaki, Takashi 34
Moriarty, Mark 130
Mornay Sauce 41
Mullins, Grainne 114
Murphy, Jess 32
Murphy, Vanessa 115
Mussel & Potato Salad 64
Mustard & Dill Butter 29

O

O'Keeffe, Grainne 113
Oreo Millionaires 121
Overnight Oats 42

P

Pancakes 46
Paneer 34
Panna Cotta 113, 114
Parsley Sauce 41
Peach Melba 110
Peppers, Stuffed 94
Peanut Cookies 108
Pine Nut Spice Butter 28
Plaice, Baked 62
Ploughman's Steak Sandwich 49
Portuguese Custard Tarts 119
Potatoes 82, 85, 86
Potato Gratin 85
Potato Straw Cake 86

R

Radish Tzatziki 48
Ranch Dressing 39, 64
Redmond, Mary 60
Rice Pudding 115, 116
Rice Pudding with Whiskey Sauce 116
Ricotta-stuffed Spatchcocked Roast Chicken 72
Ruth, Caitlin 75, 132
Ryan, Patrick 98

S

Saffron Béchamel 61
Scones, Cranberry & Blood Orange 105
Seafood Chowder 56
Seafood Crumble 66
Seaweed Butter 28
Seaweed Crackers 106
Sheep Yogurt 32
Skehan, Donal 80
Smoked Trout Pâté 58
Soured Cream 41
Spinach, Creamed 89
Split Pea & Spinach Dhal 88
Steak, Sandwich 49

T

Tabasco Butter 29
Tacos 81
Tadka Butter 29, 88
Tart, Dillisk, Leek & Cheese 93
Three Cheese Baked Gnocchi 80
Tobin, Anne Marie 94
Tortillas, Buttermilk 97
Turkey Meatballs 70
Turkish Eggs 44
Turkish Golden Yogurt 30

U

Upside-down Pancakes 46

V

Vinegar Milk 34

W

Whey 37
White Russian 134
Worcestershire Sauce and Chives Butter 29

Y

Yogurt 30
Yogurt, Turkish Golden 30

BIBLIOGRAPHY

Allen, Darina *Forgotten Skills of Cooking* (Kyle Cathie 2009)

Allen, Myrtle *The Ballymaloe Cookbook* (Gill & MacMillan 1977)

Arbuthnot, Sharon; ní Mhaonaigh, Máire; Toner, Gregory *A History of Ireland in 100 Words* (Royal Irish Academy 2019)

Berens, Abra *Ruffage* (Chronicle Books 2019)

Bertelsen, Aaron *Grow Fruit and Vegetables in Pots* (Phaidon 2020)

Boisard, Pierre *Camembert* (University of California Press 2003)

Campion Charles; Kyriakou, Theodore *Real Greek Food* (Pavilion 2000)

Casas, Penelope *The Foods & Wines of Spain* (Penguin 1985)

Cloake, Felicity *The A-Z of Eating* (Fig Tree 2016)

Dunk, Anja *Strudel, Noodles & Dumplings* (4th Estate 2018)

Edelmann, Anton; Dorelli, Peter *The Savoy Food & Drink Book* (Pyramid 1988)

Fallon, Sally *Nourishing Traditions* (NewTrends Publishing 1999)

Ferguson, Giana *Gubbeen* (Kyle 2014)

Fitzgerald, Garrett *The Brother Hubbard Cookbook* (Gill Books 2016)

Goldstein, Darra *The Georgian Feast* (University of California Press 1999)

Granger, Bill *Bills Food* (Murdoch 2002)

Granger, Bill *Sydney Food* (Murdoch 2000)

Harris, Henry *The Fifth Floor Cookbook* (4th Estate 1998)

Harvey, Graham *We Want Real Food* (Constable 2006)

Hazan, Giuliano *The Classic Pasta Cookbook* (Dorling Kindersley 1993)

Jackson, Michael *Bar & Cocktail Book* (Mitchell Beazley 1994)

Katz, Sandor Ellix *The Art of Fermentation* (Chelsea Green 2012)

Kurlansky, Mark *Milk* (Bloomsbury 2018)

Mahon, Bríd *Land of Milk & Honey* (Poolbeg 1991)

McCarthy, Patrick; Hawkes, Richard *Northside of the Mizen* (Mizen Productions 1999)

McFadden, Joshua *Six Seasons* (Artisan 2017)

McGee, Harold *On Food And Cooking* (Unwin 1986)

McKenna, Clodagh *Clodagh's Irish Kitchen* (Kyle 2015)

McMahon, Jp *The Irish Cookbook* (Phaidon 2020)

Messom, Patricia *The Stuffed Olive Cookbook* (Trish Messom 2013)

Olney, Richard *Simple French Food* (Penguin 1983)

Olney, Richard *The Good Cook: Beverages* (Time Life 1982)

Packer, Sarit; Srulovich, Itamar *Honey & Co* (Saltyard Books 2014)

Pollan, Michael *The Omnivore's Dilemma* (Penguin Press 2006)

Reed, Ben *Cool Cocktails* (Ryland Peters & Small 2000)

Rhatigan, Prannie *Irish Seaweed Kitchen* (Booklink 2009)

Roden, Claudia *A New Book of Middle Eastern Food* (Penguin 1970)

Roden, Claudia *The Food of Spain* (Michael Joseph 2012)

Sahni, Julie *Classic Indian Cooking* (Dorling Kindersley 1986)

Salaman, Redcliffe *The History and Social Influence of the Potato* (Cambridge University Press 1985)

Sexton, Regina; Cowan, Cathal *Ireland's Traditional Foods* (Teagasc 1997)

Sexton, Regina *A Little History of Irish Food* (Gill & Macmillan 1998)

Shanahan, Martin; McKenna, Sally *Irish Seafood Cookery* (Estragon 2006)

Shanahan, Martin *Martin's Fishy Fishy Cookbook* (Estragon Press 2011)

Snapes, Richard; Harrington, Grant; Hemingway, Eve *Bread and Butter* (Quadrille 2018)

Stupak, Alex; Rothman, Jordana *Tacos* (Potter 2015)

Thomson, Claire *The Art of the Larder* (Quadrille 2017)

Tosi, Christina *Momofuku Milk Bar* (Potter 2011)

Treuille, Eric; Erath, Birgit *Barbecue* (Dorling Kindersley 2000)

ACKNOWLEDGEMENTS

Jacinta Dalton is head of the Galway International Hotel School at GMIT, Galway, @jcdal • **Ahmet Dede** is chef-proprietor at Dede, Baltimore, Co Cork, @chefahmetdede • **Jess Murphy** is chef-proprietor at Kai Restaurant, Galway city, kairestaurant.ie • **Takashi Miyazaki** is chef-proprietor of Ichigo Ichie and Miyazaki in Cork city, ichigoichie.ie • **Brian McDermott** is chef-proprietor at The Foyle Hotel, Moville, Co Donegal, foylehotel.ie • **Aran McMcMahon** is chef-proprietor at Rua, Castlebar, Co Mayo, caferua.com • **Niamh Fox** cooks and farms in Co Clare, @niamhfox • **Clodagh McKenna** is a chef, author, TV presenter and columnist for *The Evening Standard,* clodaghmckenna.com • **Caitlin Ruth** operates the food truck Caitlin Ruth Food, caitlinruthfood.ie • **Donal Skehan** is a food writer, photographer and television presenter, based in Dublin, donalskehan.com • **Mary Redmond** ran Murphy Blacks Restaurant in Kilkee, Co Clare • **Tony Davidson** is chef-proprieor at Fisk Seafod Bar, Downings, Co Donegal, fiskseafoodbar.com • **Anne Marie Tobin** is a chef and food stylist, annemarietobin.com • **Patrick Ryan** runs Firehouse Bakery and Café in Delgany, Co Wicklow, thefirehouse.ie • **Dervla James** is chef-proprietor at Pudding Row, Easky, Co Sligo, puddingrow.ie • **Grainne O'Keeffe** is chef at Clanbrassil House, Dublin, @grainne43 • **Grainne Mullins** is Eurotoques Young Chef of the Year, 2019, @MullinsGrainne • **Vanessa Murphy** is chef-proprietor of Las Tapas de Lola, Dublin, lastapasdelola.com • **Darren Hogarty** is pastry chef at Chapter One Restaurant, Dublin, @StanPastry • **Trish Messom** is chef-proprietor of The Stuffed Olive, Bantry, Co Cork, @thestuffedolive • **Graham Herterich, The Cupcake Bloke**, is proprietor of The Bakery, Rialto, Dublin 8, thecupcakebloke.com • **Mark Jennings** is chef-proprietor at Pilgrims Restaurant, Roscarbery, Co Cork, pilgrims.ie • **Adrian Martin** is a chef, author and television presenter, chefadrian.ie • **Lilly Higgins** is a cookery columnist for *The Irish Times,* lillyhiggins.ie • **Mark Moriarty** is a television presenter and cooks at The Greenhouse Restaurant, Dublin, markmoriarty.ie.

The authors would like to thank: The featured dairy farming families, Cathy Curran, Lynda Thompson, Dr Marianne Walsh, Caroline Gunn; Professor Alan Kelly, Regina Sexton, Professor Patrick Wall, Kevin Sheridan, Sally O'Toole - Food Styling Assistant, Fermoyle Pottery, Andrew Law, 1010 Printing International Ltd, Anne Marie Tobin and Mike O'Toole. Connie and PJ McKenna, and all the chefs who generously contributed recipes.